D1566999

THE
SPIRIT
OF
SOLIDARITY

THE
SPIRIT
OF
SOLIDARITY

JÓZEF TISCHNER

Translated by Marek B. Zaleski
and Benjamin Fiore, S.J.

Harper & Row, Publishers, San Francisco

Cambridge, Hagerstown, New York, Philadelphia
London, Mexico City, São Paulo, Sydney

1817

FIRST EDITION

Designer: Jim Mennick

Library of Congress Cataloging in Publication Data

Tischner, Józef.
 THE SPIRIT OF SOLIDARITY.

 Translation of: Etyka Solidarności. 2nd ed. 1982.
 1. Poland—Politics and government—1980– . 2. NSZZ
"Solidarność" (Labor organization) 3. Christian ethics—Catholic
authors. I. Title.
DK4442.T5713 1984 322'.2'09438 83–48988
ISBN 0-06-068271-X

84 85 86 87 88 10 9 8 7 6 5 4 3 2 1

CONTENTS

FOREWORD

FATHER JÓZEF TISCHNER has been one of the spiritual leaders of an unusually ethical social movement. The Solidarity union in Poland is a distinctive combination not only of social classes but of ideas, held together by a transcendental belief in ultimate justice. Committed to peaceful action, Solidarity is motivated by simple religious faith.

Polish Solidarity is an alliance of workers, intellectuals, and peasants. That terminology smacks of Leninist cant. But in the case of the Solidarity Movement, unlike that of Bolshevism, it is the fact. The union has been forged by police oppression and the official big lie, both of which the Polish people rejected. That rejection has linked in a common effort to purify and democratize Polish political life the three broad strata of the increasingly modern and literate Polish society.

The Solidarity Movement is an ethical and a peaceful manifestation. It is truly a remarkable accomplishment that in the course of several years of sustained struggle against an oppressive police regime, Solidarity did not inflict a single death. More than that, in the face of repeated brutality and violence, in the face of frequent provocations, in the face even of violent beatings administered by the police to Solidarity leaders, the masses of the Solidarity Movement remained self-disciplined and dedicated to the pursuit of peaceful change. Nonviolence and even turning of the other cheek have been the lodestars of its behavior.

Solidarity's hope for a better tomorrow has been fueled by a profound belief in God. Its religious nature is spontaneous, widespread, and genuinely profound. One need only recall the pictures of the Gdańsk workers on their knees during luncheon break in order to have their confessions heard and to receive

Holy Communion. Such faith was given philosophical content by a few outstanding individuals who addressed themselves publicly to questions that truly mattered, to issues that were burning, to concerns that were intensely heartfelt.

Father Tischner has been the outstanding Church spokesman in linking theology to the quest for social justice, in making God relevant to a land that in recent history has been visited only too often by Satan. As a consequence, Father Tischner has come to be recognized as the major philosopher of the Solidarity Movement, as the churchman who truthfully and confidently expresses maxims that guide Solidarity members in their quest for a just society. In Tischner's words, "Solidarity need not be imposed upon the human being from outside, with the use of force. That virtue is born of itself, spontaneously, from the heart. . . . Solidarity is born from goodwill and causes in people goodwill." In his sermons, Father Tischner reminds his listeners, "Freedom is imperative and freedom is disturbing. Without freedom, no act, no desire, no fulfillment of a function, is the human being's own act. The human being must be himself in his acts. Where there is the absence of freedom, there the human being is not himself—even when he does what is expected of him."

Father Tischner, theologian, is also a compelling preacher on behalf of genuine democracy. In his lectures he justified the strike as an instrument for achieving social justice; he calls for a bloodless revolution in social consciousness; he urges the exercise of authority that is based above all on respect for the human being; and he exorcises national treason. He endows the concept "Let Poland be Poland" with ethical meaning by reminding those who listen to him that genuine freedom means responsibility and responsibility requires an awareness of justice.

There is power in his words, and his small book is an explosive volume. It contains ideas that in their simple truth are fundamentally antithetical to the reality of experience under Communism. Above all, there is authenticity in his thought, just as there is historical authenticity in the Solidarity phenomenon—

and that makes Father Józef Tischner a truly major figure in the Polish spiritual rebirth.

Eighteenth-century Poland, on the eve of its partition, also struggled for reforms in spite of external Russian obstruction. In so doing, it saluted one of its great reformers and thinkers by casting a special medal honoring (in Latin) "him who dared to be wise." It is truly appropriate to say similarly of Father Tischner: *"Sapere auso."*

ZBIGNIEW BRZEZINSKI
August 1983

FROM THE TRANSLATORS

For the last four years public attention around the world has been focused on a succession of events in Poland. The first visit of Pope John Paul II in 1979, the birth of Solidarity, the declaration of the state of war by the Communist junta against the Polish nation, the underground resistance, the second papal visit in 1983, and the "legalization" of the martial law measures, all attracted attention and aroused curiosity. Throughout the world, workers, people of faith, citizens living under oppressive regimes, students of the world political order, and lovers of freedom and human rights have sensed something of importance for them in these events. However, the sparsity of coverage in the public media caused by the restriction of the flow of information in and out of Poland and the preoccupation of the media with issues of politics and global power struggle allow only part of the story to emerge. The historical roots and philosophical and religious values that underlie the events in question often remain especially unclear to those little familiar with the former and current experiences of Poland. All of these result in deep differences, and occasionally overt misconceptions, in understanding the sources, ideals, and workings of the Solidarity Movement. The Movement represents for some a political party, for others a social or nationalistic upheaval, and for still others merely a trade union.

Father Tischner—the witness of the birth and growing pains of Solidarity and now the witness of its tragedy and suffering—with the skill of a scholar and teacher, and with the love of a spiritual father and a Pole—takes us behind the outward appearances. He shows convincingly and authoritatively how far back in history, how deeply in the hearts and minds of the people, Solidarity is rooted. Even more importantly, he shows the reader that the roots and principles of Solidarity span geographic, religious, national, and economic borders.

One could attempt to evaluate Father Tischner's book from a variety of points of view—scholastic, literary, or emotional. However, it seems that the author himself introduced and most accurately characterized the book when he wrote, "I wanted . . . to fulfill the duty of a Christian philosopher and to accompany the events with light from the words of wisdom of philosophers." Indeed, the book is a guiding light for all who are concerned with understanding what is behind the dramatic events unfolding in contemporary Poland and who want to enter into dialogue with the ethical implications of these events for their own lives and for human rights everywhere in the world.

With this in mind, we translators seized the opportunity to make this book accessible to the English-speaking audience. As educators, we ourselves are concerned to reflect on and to enhance justice and human rights and to direct our students toward this reflection and action. As members of the Solidarity and Human Rights Association, we have committed our energy to awakening people of openness and goodwill to the ideals of the Solidarity Movement and their impact on the state of justice and human rights in the contemporary world. The translation of this book is one part of our effort. We sincerely believe and hope that readers will derive from the pages of this book as much joy and wisdom as we did from working on the translation. If they do, we shall consider ourselves rewarded beyond measure.

Although we have tried to do our best to preserve the beauty and flavor of the original text, we do realize that it is often difficult to convey in a translation each and every nuance and subtlety of the text. (For example, we occasionally altered the original Polish expressions in the interest of nonexclusionary language.) For any flaws, we apologize to the author and to the reader.

We dedicate our work to all people of goodwill, but above all to all those who, *regardless* of their place of residence and nationality, have become prisoners of conscience and victims of oppression for their action taken in defense of one or another form of human solidarity. We want to dedicate our work to all who suffer imprisonment or exile or must live under the threat of it. Among the latter are the well-known as well as countless unnamed members of the Solidarity Movement, whose tireless self-sacrifice, principled restraint, profound reflection, and fearless action have given the Polish nation and the world a challenging model of a peaceful quest in the noble cause of human dignity and freedom.

Finally, we wish to express our gratitude to all those who helped us in our undertaking. Specifically, our gratitude is due to Mrs. and Mr. Elżbieta and Andrzej Cyran, who called our attention to Father Tischner's book. We are also grateful to Dr. Roger K. Cunningham, who helped us to achieve a smooth and consistent translation, and to Ms. Rosalind J. Forse, who typed and retyped the manuscript. Our special thanks are addressed to Dr. Zbigniew Brzezinski, who confirmed the value of our effort with his Foreword. Last, but not least, we owe thanks to the publishers: on the one hand, Harper & Row, Publishers, Inc., and especially Mr. John Loudon, who had the vision and courage to undertake the task of editing and publishing this book in English and Ms. Virginia Rich for her helpful copy editing of the manuscript: on the other hand, Editions Spotkania and Mr. Piotr Jegliński, who granted permission for the translation. The list would not be complete without conveying our thanks to Father Józef Tischner himself for his approval of our initiative and his words of encouragement.

MAREK B. ZALESKI, M.D., Ph.D.
School of Medicine
State University of New York, Buffalo

BENJAMIN FIORE, S.J., Ph.D.
Canisius College, Buffalo

SOLIDARITY OF CONSCIENCES

(A sermon delivered in Wawel, October 19, 1980)

Then Jesus told his disciples a parable to teach them that they should always pray and never become discouraged. "In a certain town there was a judge who neither feared God nor respected man. And there was a widow in that same town who kept coming to him and pleading for her rights, saying, 'Help me against my opponent!' For a long time the judge refused to act, but at last he said to himself, 'Even though I don't fear God or respect man, yet because of all the trouble this widow is giving me, I will see to it that she gets her rights. If I don't she will keep on coming and finally wear me out!'

And the Lord continued, "Listen to what that corrupt judge said. Now, will God not judge in favor of his own people who cry to him day and night for help? Will he be slow to help them? I tell you, he will judge in their favor and do it quickly. But will the Son of Man find faith on earth when he comes?" (Luke 18:1–8).*

TODAY, we are bringing to Wawel Hill[1†] the problems that are closest to our hearts, problems that are summarized in a single word—*solidarity.* The word *solidarity* concentrates in itself our uncertain hopes, full of trepidation; it stimulates us to heroism and reflection; and it binds together people who only yesterday were far apart. History creates words in order that, in turn, they may create history. The word *solidarność* has joined

---

*Scripture quotations in this chapter are taken from Today's English Version of the Bible.

†Notes explaining historical and cultural references have been provided at the end of the book.

other, very Polish words to give new form to our days. Here are just some of these words: *freedom, independence, human dignity*—and today, *solidarity*. Each of us feels the awesome gravity of meaning within this word. Bearing this weight we stand today on Wawel Hill among the tombs of the Piasts[2] and the Jagiellons,[3] by the ashes of Mickiewicz[4] and Słowacki,[5] in front of the altar of the Son of God.

The gospel of Christ—the good news—comes forth to greet us. What is the gospel telling us today? It tells us about a single thing, the power of faith and prayer. Let us listen to the words of the gospel:

> And the Lord continued, "Listen to what that corrupt judge said. Now, will God not judge in favor of his own people who cry to him day and night for help? Will he be slow to help them? I tell you, he will judge in their favor and do it quickly. But will the Son of Man find faith on earth when he comes?"

This is the gospel for today. These words have approached us. They speak of the power and greatness of the human being, of the ways to use God's omnipotence for human well-being and happiness. One must have faith; God serves those who trust him. And here we discover the character of this encounter between us, with the burden contained in the wonderful word *solidarity,* and the gospel, with its call for an unshakable faith.

Let us look briefly at the burden we are carrying. This old but also very new word *solidarity,* what does it mean? To what does it call us? What memories does it bring back? To explicate more precisely its meaning, perhaps it is necessary to reach into the gospel and seek the origin of the word there. Christ explains its meaning: "Carry one another's burden and in this way fulfill God's law" (paraphrase of Paul in Gal. 6:2). What does it mean to be in solidarity? It means to carry the burden of another person. No one is an island all alone. We are bound to each other even if we do not know it. The landscape binds us, flesh and blood bind us, work and speech bind us. However, we are not always conscious of these bonds. When solidarity is born, this consciousness is awakened, and then speech and word appear— and at that point something that was hidden becomes manifest. All our bonds become visible. Then one person shoulders the burden of another. Solidarity speaks, calls, cries, undertakes sacrifice. Then the burden of one's fellow human often becomes greater than one's own. In this way the disciple of Christ fulfills His law.

Solidarity has still another facet; solidarity does not need to be imposed from the outside by force. This virtue is born of itself, spontaneously, from the heart. Did anybody force the Good Samaritan to bend over the wounded man who lay by the roadside? The Good Samaritan helped his fellow man because such was his goodwill. The virtue of solidarity is an expression of human goodwill. In essence we all are in solidarity, because in the depth of our souls we are people of goodwill. Solidarity is born out of goodwill and awakens the goodwill in human beings. It is like a warm ray of sun; wherever the ray falls, it leaves a warmth that radiates spontaneously. Solidarity is concerned with only one thing: that no one put obstacles before it—stupid, nonsensical obstacles.

And one more thing—solidarity, the one that is born from the pages and the spirit of the gospel, does not need an enemy or opponent to strengthen itself and to grow. It turns toward all and not against anyone. The foundation and the source of solidarity lies in whatever constitutes a true goal in the life of each person. When spring comes, the goal is to sow and plow on time. When autumn comes, the goal is to harvest on time. When a house is on fire, the goal is to put out the fire. For a teacher, the goal is that the school be a true school; the university, a true university; the book, a true book. For all of us the goal is that the truth mean always the truth; and justice, justice. It is necessary to clean house. Indeed, the imperative for this unifies and stirs us to action. It unifies more deeply and more permanently than the fear of enemies. We want to be a unified nation, but not unified by fear. We want the simplest human duty to unify us.

Today we are living through unusual times. People are discarding their masks; they are emerging from their hiding places and showing their true faces. From under the dust and out of oblivion their consciences are emerging. Today we are as we truly are. Believers are believers, doubters are doubters, and nonbelievers, nonbelievers. There is no point in assuming someone else's role. Everyone wants to be called by his or her own name. What we are living through is not only a social or economic event but one that above all touches us personally. The problem impinges upon human dignity, human dignity that is based on the conscience of human beings. The deepest solidarity is solidarity of consciences.

Today's gospel asks each of us, "But will the Son of Man find faith on earth when he comes?" Will he find faith? The key to our cause is faith.

Today, we are on Wawel Hill to strengthen our faith, to strengthen it primarily through prayer. Here lie the ashes of those who, above all, *have had faith.* How much faith must Saint Stanisław[6] have had when he excommunicated the cruel king.[7] Perhaps, as he has been accused, by doing so he undermined the power of the young kingdom. Bishop Stanisław believed that he did not undermine but built up this power. How much faith must King Jagiełło[8] have had when he marched to Grunwald[9] to fight against the knighthood of almost the whole of Europe. What prayer grew out of this faith! This entire edifice[10] is built out of prayers. Finally, there is the faith of John Paul II, until not long ago the master of this house. These walls also contain his prayer. We remember how he spoke to us, "You must be strong by the strength of faith. You must be faithful. Today you need this strength more than in any other period of history." The faith is here. When the Son of Man comes he shall find faith. We are here to add our own prayer to the prayer of history, to add to the awesome faith of history our small faith—faith as small as the seed of the mustard tree (Luke 17:6).

Let me touch upon one more thing. I know that the place upon which we stand is so great and so sacred that in the face of it all contemporary human names are belittled and vanish. But solidarity also represents our gratitude. We pray today together with the workers of Gdańsk,[11] Szczecin,[12] and other cities of Poland, who came here to pay homage to the memory of kings. This is a good occasion to say what every praying person feels. I shall say it with one phrase: We are thankful. We are thankful for our solidarity of consciences. We wish to be grateful because this too is solidarity, "Carry the burden of each other. . . ." Let us take upon ourselves today the burden of heartfelt prayer.

> "Now, will God not judge in favor of his own people who cry to him day and night for help? Will he be slow to help them? I tell you, he will judge in their favor and do it quickly."

———

COMMUNION

WE HAVE faced the task of more deeply understanding the solidarity idea. Let us focus our attention on the little word *idea*. Solidarity, of which we wish to speak, is neither a concept nor a ready-made ethical theory; it is an idea. Usually, concepts lend themselves to a relatively easy definition, whereas ideas always remain to some extent undefined. Ideas are more models of things than expressions of their actual state. Solidarity for us is something to pattern after, something that defines itself as it is realized, and something that must be constantly redefined. It is also not connected with any ready-made theory. A theory is a system of justification in which one thing is tied to another and the one thing justifies the other. An idea is something that essentially does not need justification; it justifies itself.

Why solidarity? No answer to this question can supply a justification. One can only say, "Solidarity, because this is the right way." An idea is like some sort of light. Light shines on its own; it "justifies" itself. If we walk along the shadows we reach light. Every shadow extends behind itself, but light has nowhere further to extend.

Nevertheless, solidarity requires further understanding. One has to ask, What does solidarity say to us? A person is always in solidarity with someone and for someone. But then, with whom is our solidarity to be, and for whom? Pursuing this line of questioning, one might also ask, Through what acts and deeds can solidarity express itself?

My task here is not to give advice or to formulate prohibitions or directives; it is something more essential, that is, an examination of the area of life that is illuminated by the idea of solidarity. These reflections have ethical character, and the principal task of ethics is to accompany human beings on the path of life and to point out unequivocally, as much as possible, the values among which they are destined to proceed. After a person has seen the world of values that surround him, he himself is capable of formulating prohibitions and directives; he himself is able to counsel himself; and when the need arises, he is also able to evaluate himself. Today, I would like to draw attention to two key values—the human conscience and the natural bond of human beings with those who suffer.

The ethic of solidarity intends to be an ethic of conscience. It assumes that human beings are endowed with conscience. Conscience denotes the natural human "ethical sense," a sense that, to a significant degree, is independent of the various ethical systems. We have many ethical systems, but our conscience is one and the same. Conscience is prior to those systems. Conscience constitutes an independent reality within an individual, something like the mind and the will. We can exercise our will and mind, or we can neglect to exercise them. Likewise, we can listen to our conscience, stifle it, or even deny it. Conscience is a voice that calls within us. To what does the conscience of today summon humankind? It calls above all for people to want to have a conscience.

We realize the risk we are taking when we assert that the ethic of solidarity intends to be an ethic of conscience. What if it turns out that people have mistaken consciences? Would it not be safer to pay no attention to conscience but rather to concentrate on writing road signs and putting them up along the path of life? Certainly, this would be safer. This, however, is not a way to build human morality. It is not a question of a military drill but of behavior that issues from within. In order for road signs to build morality they must be accepted by conscience. Conscience is the knack of reading the road signs. Only conscience knows which road sign one should turn attention to, here and now. Christian thinkers have been saying, Conscience is the voice of God. This means a God who does not speak through the human conscience is not a true God but an idol. The true God first touches conscience.

A person—even one who errs but still has some conscience—will certainly recognize his errors eventually and is then capable of changing. A person without conscience is incapable of this. Even when such a person does change, it is because the circumstances have changed and he is forced to adapt to them.

It is impossible to be in solidarity with people who have no conscience.

With people without conscience one may ride the train, sit at table during supper, read a book—this, however, is not yet solidarity. Not every "we," not every "together," is of itself solidarity. Authentic solidarity—let us repeat it once more—is solidarity of consciences. This is clear because to be in solidarity with a person means to rely on that person, and to rely on a person means to believe that there is something permanent in a person, something that does not fail. For this, however, one thing is needed: one must want to have a conscience. Primarily those who want a conscience are those who already have a conscience.

This is sad, because it seems that human beings have the power to destroy in themselves the very thing that determines their humanity. But it is also joyful, because it turns out that conscience can be restored if only one wants it.

Solidarity is the creation not only of those who have always had conscience but also of those who have restored it in themselves.

The ethic of solidarity develops and expresses itself in a particular social system, in a particular time and place. Solidarity is a solidarity with people and for people; thus, it is a social phenomenon. It carries within itself certain consequences. Among others, this question arises, What are the bonds connecting the phenomenon of solidarity with politics? Let us consider the matter with a concrete example.

Take the parable of the Good Samaritan; he also lived in a particular society, in a world of a particular religion and politics. Nonetheless, his deed somehow breached the limits of this world, reached beyond the structures that this world imposed upon people. The good deed of the Samaritan was a response to the specific cry of a specific man. It is simple; someone is crying for help. A wounded man lies in a roadside ditch, and his pain has a particular character. It is not the result of disease, unfortunate coincidence, advanced age; rather, it is pain caused by someone else. It was one man who devised this lot for another. It is precisely this fact that is of importance; it is this that in a particular way stirs conscience and calls for solidarity. Nothing outrages one more than a gratuitous wound, a wound inflicted on one person by another. We have sympathy for a patient who has undergone surgery. For someone who has been mistreated we have sympathy, but at the very same time we are outraged. From the spectacle of such pain a particularly deep solidarity is born.

With whom, therefore, is our solidarity? It is, above all, with those who have been wounded by other people, with those who suffer pain that could be avoided—accidental, needless pain.

This does not preclude solidarity with others, with all who suffer. However, the solidarity with those who suffer at the hands of others is particularly vital, strong, spontaneous.

Does this touch politics? Yes, indeed; but only when the politics is corrupt. When the politics is good, it is permeated of itself with the spirit of solidarity. Is it not the aim of politics to organize the arena of human life in such a way that one person does not inflict injury on another? When faithful to itself, politics builds a space in which the consciences of Samaritans can act. Nobody should fear such consciences; it is not the fire brigade but the fire itself that is dangerous. The Good Samaritan does not even pursue the robbers to capture them. His first duty is to care for the wounds of the stricken one. Those who are in politics will take care of the wrongdoers. Solidarity is a closeness—it is a brotherly feeling for those who have been struck down.

Let us put together the major thoughts. Conscience is the foundation of solidarity, and the stimulus for its development is the cry for help from someone wounded by another human being. Solidarity establishes specific, interpersonal bonds; one person joins with another to tend to the one who needs care. I am with you, you are with me, we are together—for him. We—for him. We, not to look at each other, but for him. Which comes first here? Is "we" first, or is "for him" first? The communion of solidarity differs from many other communions in that "for him" is first and "we" comes later. First is the wounded one and the cry of pain. Later, conscience speaks, since it is able to hear and understand this cry. This is all it takes for communion to spring up.

DIALOGUE

DIALOGUE means that people have come out of their hiding places, have approached each other, and have begun to exchange opinions. The very beginning of a dialogue—coming out of hiding—is itself a big event. One must reach out, cross the threshold, offer one's hand, and find a common place for conversation. This place will no longer be a hiding place where one remains alone with one's fear; rather, it will be a place of meeting, a beginning of something common, perhaps the beginning of a home. How many hurdles must one clear in the course of time to begin a dialogue. How much patience, in order to continue a dialogue. Not only is it necessary to overcome fear, to remove prejudices, but it is also necessary to find a language that means the same for both parties. It cannot be the language of a particular group, much less a language of insinuations, of slander, and it surely cannot be a language of accusation. "Let what you say be simply 'yes' or 'no'; anything more than this comes from evil" (Matt. 5:37). The language of honest dialogue is an "objective" language, that is, a language that corresponds to objects. Black is called black; white is called white. No one tries to manufacture pleasure out of pain.

Not every conversation between people is an honest dialogue. Honest dialogue causes a true revolution in people's lives and in the life of a society. It is like letting light into the darkness of a cellar. Very often truth is compared to light that "enlightens everyone who comes into this world" (John 1:9). Dialogue, by bringing light, unveils the truth. In other words, it restores the proper appearance to things and events.

Solidarity is always a solidarity of some sort of dialogue. What does this mean, on closer scrutiny?

An honest dialogue grows up from a secure foundation that must be accepted—explicitly or implicitly—by both sides; neither you nor I can know the truth about each other if we remain at a distance from one another, closed inside the walls of our fears. No, we must look at ourselves as if from the outside, I with your eyes and you with mine. In conversation we must compare what we see, and only in this way are we in a position to find the answer to the question of how it really is with us. As long as I look at myself exclusively with my own eyes, I know only part of the truth. As long as you look at yourself with your own eyes, you, too, know only part of the truth. Likewise, when I look at you and consider only what I myself see and when you look at me and take into account only what you see, both of us are subject to a partial illusion. The full truth is the fruit of our experiences in common—yours about me and mine about you. Common views are the fruits of exchanged points of view. Thus, dialogue—honest dialogue—can be understood not merely as a way in which people conduct themselves but as a necessary means to achieve social truth.

The first condition of dialogue is an ability to "feel" the point of view of another. It is not simply a question of compassion but of something more—the recognition that someone else, from his point of view, is always to some extent right. No one spontaneously shuts himself up in a hiding place; obviously one must have a reason. One must recognize and accept this reason. In the first words of a dialogue there is hidden the acknowledgment that "certainly you are to some extent right." Coupled with this comes another, no less important declaration: "certainly I am not entirely right." By these avowals both sides rise, as it were, above themselves, reaching for a common and single point of view on things and events. When I undertake a dialogue I am thereby ready to make the personal truth of someone else a part of my truth about that someone and to make the truth about me a part of someone else's truth. Dialogue is a building of reciprocity.

The question arises, however: a dialogue, *about what?* There are so many truths about the universe, about humanity, about things and events. Is there not a need for some sort of hierarchy of importance? We are going to keep our discussion here focused on the ethic of solidarity that has become a burning issue in recent months. What constitutes the main theme of the dialogue that grows out of the ethics of solidarity?

Generally speaking, it is suffering—the suffering of one human being caused by another. This kind of suffering rouses a particular indignation. Each person has enough suffering allotted by nature itself—diseases, infirmities, death. Another person should not introduce onto this burden additional pain. Rather, one should aim at lightening the cross that is carried by one's fellow human beings. Our tragedy is that very often the opposite happens; such pain—needless pain, inflicted at the hand of a fellow human being—is particularly repugnant and spontaneously evokes protest from people of good will.

But this is still too general. Our present-day ethos of solidarity is more concrete. It was born among workers to free human work from needless pain. Work is one of the natural human burdens. One must bear it, as fate decrees: "Anyone who would not work, should not eat" (2 Thess. 3:10). This means, however, that to the natural pains connected with work no needless pains should be added—pains inflicted at the hands of another. This pain has been described in a variety of ways; the word *exploitation* is most commonly used. This is a good word, but it should refer to concrete reality, suffering—the suffering of a worker coming from the hands of his or her neighbor.

The dialogue of solidarity is about this very pain. Everything else is secondary. This pain gives the words of solidarity their greatest power of persuasion. This is why the cry of solidarity is particularly far-reaching. When discourse about it moves away from its fundamental theme, the power of persuasion wanes and the voice does not resound as widely.

An honest dialogue is always concerned with the truth. The dialogue of solidarity—the dialogue of awakened consciences—is concerned, above all, with the theme of the needless suffering of working people. The truth must be concrete, as concrete as the suffering itself. It should bring an answer to the simplest questions of the people: Where does suffering come from, and how can it be avoided?

The suffering of the worker gives high moral standing to the words of solidarity. These are not ordinary human words; they are not even the words of complaint; they are, above all, the words of testimony. For us to go through the world of suffering of the worker and to give testimony—this is the solidarity of consciences. Giving testimony means, first of all, to call things by their right names, to use language that fits the objects. Giving testimony also means evoking in people an opposition to the needless pain of the worker. From either meaning emerges the key question concerning dialogue: What to do to eliminate this pain? The answer does not come easy, but in the final analysis one thing is particularly precious here: hope. Hope is awakening that things and events can be changed. The people involved in the dialogue about solidarity must guard this hope as the apple of their eye.

WORK

THE SIGNIFICANCE we give today to the idea of solidarity is in a particular way bound to the reality of human work. Solidarity turns out to be a communion of working people who strive to free human work from the hardships and suffering caused by other human beings, that is, from hardships that are not inherent in the process of converting raw materials into a product. Work is an axis of solidarity. When considering the ethics of solidarity one cannot bypass the question of the essence of work; moreover, such a consideration must be seen as a key issue of these ethics.

Writers have treated the essence of work from various angles. This is neither the time nor the place to analyze the strengths and weaknesses of those dissertations. What I am going to say here is directly associated with ethics; therefore, it is no wonder that I must step beyond the limits of strictly economic and sociological descriptions of the concept of work. My aim is to capture the basic idea of work and, with this as a prism, perhaps to see better what role work plays in human life, to see what position work occupies in the hierarchy of human values.

What is work? I answer: Work is a particular form of interpersonal conversation that serves to sustain and develop human life. Even briefer: Work is a conversation in the service of life. But this matter requires an explanation.

Work is a particular form of conversation. In ordinary conversation people exchange words among themselves, that is, they exchange various sounds imbued with meaning. From words, sentences are built; from sentences, the entire story. From the exchange of meaningful sounds—words—one person grows to understand another. Working people do something similar. The objects of their exchange are not ordinary words (although this also may happen) but other products of work that in their structure are similar to words. Just as words are the synthesis of the raw material of the senses (for example, sound) with a meaning, so the product of work is a synthesis of some kind of raw material (for example, clay, ore, or iron) with a meaning (as results of this come pots, hardware, plows). Owing to work, raw material acquires a meaning. The individual meanings of things fuse, overlap, touch, and form the general world of the products of work. Only the one who is capable of grasping the meaning of these products knows how to behave in this world.

I must make a reservation. I am not talking about what work was in the times when a lone man chased a wild beast, killed it with a club made by himself, and then merely satisfied his hunger. Perhaps at those times work was not a conversation. (But was there really such a time?) Let us not speak about what has been but about what is now. Today, farmers sow seeds into land that their forefathers cleared; they reap grain with a scythe or a machine that was made somewhere in a factory; they transport the harvest to the mill where someone will make flour; flour will reach a bakery where bread is made—a food that serves life. To make all this possible, there has to be a social agreement. The very concept of agreement presupposes the existence of some kind of conversation.

The conversation of work has a wide reach. Let us note: forefathers prepared the field, workers made the scythe, a baker baked the bread, and a poet consumed it. By working I am joining the conversation that was already in progress before I was born. I am a link between the past and the future. I am an heir of the work. I am also a link in the present between those who dig out the ore and those who buy the bread. The fruit of my work reaches into the future; someone will inherit my work and its fruit. The dialogue of work goes further than an ordinary conversation. It encompasses ever larger circles of people who often do not know each other personally.

Each conversation conceals in itself a certain wisdom. Work has an inner wisdom, peculiar and appropriate to itself. This wisdom imposes demands on people, determines for them a proper "level." Everyone must know what one ought to do in order that an organic whole might grow from fragmentary work. The wisdom of work—wisdom that is incarnated not only in the human brain but also in the entire human body—results in the natural wisdom of working people. Today, the beginnings of this wisdom must be learned in school, but it is finally achieved only when, through actual work, it "gets into our blood."

The conversation of work serves basic aims—it serves life. One cannot consider the ethical aspect of work in isolation from the values associated with human life. What is life? We do not know this precisely, but we sense it well enough. When life is threatened by death, we feel it especially well; then life is what we ourselves defend. We see at that time that this is a basic value for us. It is not our highest value, since under some circumstances people are ready to sacrifice their lives for other, higher values. Nonetheless, it is a basic value, since only by "being alive" can we strive toward the higher values that are said to "give meaning to life." Work either serves life, when it sustains life and guarantees its development (the work of a farmer, a physician, a house builder, etc.), or gives a deeper meaning to life (for example, the work of an artist, a philosopher, a priest).

Thanks to the value of life that is served by work, work acquires its own value and dignity. Therefore, human activity that brings death instead of serving life is not work. No one will consider as work the extermination of people in a concentration camp or the belligerent pursuits of invaders who prefer to rob rather than work. The betrayal by Judas, even though he received remuneration, was not work. The measure of work is the human life served by that work.

Work that brings atrophy, disease, and death, instead of life, is sick work or simply not work at all. Work becomes sick or ceases to be work when the natural burden of work—the struggle of worker with raw materials—becomes multipled by another human being who was supposed to be a co-worker. In such a situation it is customary to speak about exploitation of one person by another. Exploited work, instead of creating, divides, and by dividing threatens to kill.

I said at the outset that work is a particular form of person-to-person conversation. The product of human work grows from an agreement and serves this agreement. The fruit of work is like a word journeying through time and space.

If this is the case, then we have acquired an important reference point from which to appraise the moral value of actual human work. As speech may be true or false, so, too, may work be. Not only speech can be called "true" but also work; the value of truth refers to work as it does to speech. True speech is speech that is consistent with reality, speech that grows from an agreement and promotes this agreement. True work is work that truly serves life and also grows from an agreement and continues it.

The immediate aim of work is some sort of fruit—a product. This fruit is like a word spoken at the proper moment. Work, by creating fruit that is like words, broadens the horizon of human understanding. People, in order to work and collaborate, must somehow be mutually "in the truth"—no one can lie through work to one's neighbor, because then the work would be like mumbling. Work that lies—this is exploitation. Beginning to realize that there is exploitation is like feeling the pain of a lie.

———

EXPLOITATION

JUST AS a lie is a disease of speech, exploitation is a disease of work. What is exploitation? None of the theories of exploitation that I am familiar with appears to me satisfactory. Some of these are too closely associated with systems of political economy and too loosely with ethics. Others, although actually referring to ethics, do so in an abstract way that does not reach the realm of significance. Theories do not keep up with real life. It is likely that, along with the social and economic changes that affect work in society, the nature of exploitation changes, too. Thus, when somehow we succeed in defining one prevalent form of exploitation it is replaced by another form, not yet dealt with by any theory. The question of exploitation requires repeated reflection. However, before we start "unmasking" the cases of exploitation that occur here and there, we must realize its essence. Thus, once again—What is exploitation?

Let us first call upon the natural consciousness of working people. This consciousness recognizes exploitation relatively easily. The basic sign of exploitation is *needless suffering*. Such suffering does not result from the natural resistance of raw materials but is, indirectly or directly, someone else's doing—someone somehow associated with me. When barren land forces the farmer to increase effort, there is no exploitation in this. However, if this is caused by another person, there is, in that, some sort of exploitation.

The connection between suffering and exploitation is not always totally clear-cut. It is not obvious whose suffering and which suffering is in question. Most frequently, exploitation results in the suffering of the working person, but it may also cause the pain of one who receives the fruit of work. Suffering is not always physical, but can be spiritual—for example, experiencing the senselessness of work. And all this does not preclude the possibility of exploitation without conscious pain. Nonetheless, the fact of suffering is particularly eloquent. Suffering elicits rebellion, triggers a recurring question, prompts understanding of its causes.

To understand better the essence of exploitation, we must once again recall the analogy between speech and work. A lie is a sickness of speech as exploitation is of work. If so, let us ask a key question: What relationships among people are created by work and what do the potential disturbances of such relationships look like?

First, attention should be focused upon two "vertical" relationships: the relationship to a basic project of work in society and the relationship to a particular employer.

The basic project of work is the general plan of work in a given society, which is essential at a particular point in time. Let us say that in a certain state the government projects the need for a specific quantity and quality of work, for example, the work of the miner, farmer, teacher, or physician. It is anticipated that at a given time the society will need so many physicians, teachers, miners. . . . Such a plan of work is not a matter of the individual whim of a planner. It depends on various objective factors: the natural resources of the country, its climate, its technical progress, and so on. Still, within certain limits, people have the freedom to plan. From this freedom comes the possibility of error. The basic project allots to the members of society, somewhat from above, the major directions of their choice of work. Some undertake higher education, others limit themselves to primary education; some search for happiness in industry, others in agriculture; and so forth.

The relationship to a particular employer also has a vertical character. Usually, it expresses itself as a contract in which one side promises to the other side a specified quantity and quality of work and receives in return a promise of just compensation. Thus the general project of work takes concrete shape. The exchange of services is born. The criterion of exchange becomes a principle of justice; give to everyone what is rightfully his. Product for product, merchandise for merchandise, work for work.

For ethics, one additional element is particularly important, people. The relationships mentioned above are, in fact, relationships of people with people. It is a person who authors the basic project, and it is a person who defines the content of the contract. If some error appears in the basic project, in terms of ethics it will always mean that a person has erred. Could that person have avoided the error? If someone does not live up to an accepted obligation it means that a human being has failed. Could that person have avoided this? Here, everything is by people and for people. The dimension of work is like the dimension of speech.

Along with the vertical relationships go horizontal relationships. These may be described by the expression "with someone—for someone." Work is always with someone and for someone; someone will utilize its fruits.

Cooperation consists in common participation in one and the same activity. Someone drew blueprints, someone else cut lumber, someone else made bricks. On a certain day, many knowledgeable and skilled people put the parts together into a single whole, and in this way a house was built. The house is a common creation. If the parts of the house could speak, they would tell a story about those who fashioned them and erected the house.

The house is for me, for you, for someone. The fruit of work is essentially designated for human beings. It ought to serve their life, sustain it, develop it, give it deeper meaning. Accepting the fruit of work from the hands of another or others, I should give them in exchange the fruit of my work. The principle of justice returns to everyone what is rightfully his.

Human beings are also essential within the sphere of horizontal relations; the ethical view requires us always to consider people. Regardless of how far away a co-worker and a recipient of the fruit of my work live, even if my relations with them are extremely indirect—always these are relations with human beings, whether with one or with many. For this reason, of all the words used here, the most important is the little word *for*—for someone. It shows us a meaning of work that is similar to the meaning of speech.

Work is a form of service to humankind.

Against this background, what then is exploitation? We are concerned here only with the definition, not with specific facts. Only after we have a "definition" may we ask about facts. We will try to answer the question: exploitation is the disturbance of the basic— vertical and horizontal—structures of the dialogue of work. It is this that lies at the basis of the very thought-provoking consciousness of pain and suffering of working people. Together with the consciousness of pain, the conviction is born that the pain is needless, that it could have been avoided. There is nothing so simple as to pass from disagreement to agreement. If this, which is so simple, does not happen, the question arises, Who is guilty?

I shall call the disturbance of the structure of the dialogue of work understood in this way the *moral exploitation of work*. The concept of moral exploitation of work has a broad meaning. A particular case is exploitation understood as unjust compensation for work.

Moral exploitation of work is associated with a situation of some sort of untruth in which working people find themselves. The natural agreement among them has broken down. The basic project of work went one way, and their actual work went another. The work contract has not borne reciprocity. An incomprehensible darkness separates one person from another. The event of the tower of Babel is repeated, but this time at the level of work.

Where is the beginning of falsehood? Is it in the basic project? Is it in the contract? Is it in cooperation? Or, perhaps, the little word *for* became obliterated. Could it be that "work for man" has been replaced by "man for work"? In the situation of untruth, these are the questions that are posed by the mind and conscience—the thinking conscience of a worker.

SUFFERING

Sufferings are unequal; a toothache is different from the pain caused by the death of a loved one. For working people the most obvious sign of the moral exploitation of work is their somewhat special suffering. It is neither fatigue—a normal accompaniment to overcoming the resistance of raw materials— nor hunger nor fear nor anxiety about tomorrow. These sufferings may accompany the pain of exploitation, but they do not constitute its essence. Besides, these sufferings likewise appear outside of the sphere of work. The pain of the exploited one is, above all, a moral pain. Exploitation causes a pain similar to that inflicted by a lie or by treachery.

Precise thinking requires that one always use unequivocal concepts. This also applies to the concept of exploitation. However, each attempt at precision may result in the dissociation of the concept from its content of direct experience. Formal scientific definitions of the concept of exploitation are surely very much needed, but unfortunately, they do not demonstrate what is particularly important for exploited people, their pain—needless, nonsensical, avoidable pain. I want to focus particular attention on this pain.

Occasionally, people say "abuse" instead of "exploitation." There is a bread knife on the table. A man grabs the knife and points it at someone. We then say, "He abused the knife." We speak about abuse when some object—most often a tool—is used for some end other than that for which it is intended by its nature or design. Someone "exploits" the natural goodness of a tool and makes improper use of it. The tool, however, does not know what is happening to it; it does not have a consciousness of its own. It is different with a human being. A human being feels and knows. Human beings are conscious that something wrong is being done with them.

We say, "moral exploitation of work." There is in this expression the idea that exploitation pertains first to the work and, through work, to the entire person. Anyone who "exploits" work "exploits" a human being, since it is virtually impossible to separate a human being from his or her work. Exploited work is "abused" work—an exploited person is an "abused" person.

Whenever the consciousness of moral exploitation occurs and grows, the conviction that work is something particularly valuable, something "naturally good," also becomes increasingly obvious. This is a significant association. The greater exploitation becomes, the fewer the doubts that work is something good. On a background of darkness a spark becomes a huge light; by the same kind of contrast, by experiencing the abuse of work we see more clearly its essential value.

What does this goodness point out? Where does it come from?

The natural goodness of work comes from the fact that work is a basic arena of human activity in which human goodwill expresses itself. It is not true that work represents a mere consequence of the pressure of a need. From such a pressure only gluttony and struggle are born. Only an animal is driven directly by need; this is why it chases its prey, kills, and devours it. But this is not yet work. A human being behaves differently; only humankind works. Human beings work when they suspend their needs, delay the moment of eating, when they initiate a dialogue with other human beings. People work not so much out of need as from good will. In every human work—even that which serves to satisfy needs—there is a speck of human good will. We know that good will can express itself in a variety of ways, through love, through extending a hand, through feelings of brotherhood. It also expresses itself through work. Thanks to this, work acquires a human face.

The natural goodness of work is a participation in the goodness of human will. It is the spark that bears witness to the flame.

We say, "This suffering has a moral character." What does this mean? Moral suffering does not preclude physical suffering; often these are interconnected. However, moral suffering is something different, distinct, and specific. To tiredness, fatigue, and exhaustion, to menacing hunger, something else is added, like a dull burden, a pain of the soul, a pressure on the heart.

In the perhaps not too elegant but pointedly fit language of the street, one says, "I was left dangling in the breeze" or "They made an ass of me" or "They played me for a fool." One human being has abused another, treated that person improperly, contrary to the rules of true dialogue. Something went differently than it should have. From there comes a painful feeling of disappointment, the realization of something's being "useless," a foretaste of the absurd. Is it worthwhile working with someone else? Is it worthwhile sacrificing oneself for someone? Apparently everything ends on the garbage pile.

That is not all. The pain bores deeper. Work is an expression of human goodwill. The one who "exploits" and "abuses" work is aiming at what is most human in a person—at the very goodness of human will. What an absurdity—as if ill will were something on which one could build. Exploitation aims at human goodwill by demeaning it, belittling it, betraying it. Exploitation is a form of betrayal of humankind. An exploited person feels like a betrayed person—and has every right to feel this way. To hold something in contempt means to trample it into the mud. Neither hunger nor tiredness nor physical exhaustion is the worst. The worst thing is the sullen gust of treachery that disquiets each working day, each working hour.

Perhaps now we see better what—besides an abstract definition—moral exploitation of work is. Consciousness of exploitation is, above all, an ethical type of consciousness, a kind of moral self-knowledge of man. One can evidently write a great deal about the economic aspects of exploitation, but one should not forget that in the final analysis the problem is not only an economic one. It concerns not only what happens to the product, but what happens to a human being. Human beings can withstand many physical burdens, suffer hunger, and even sacrifice their lives, but they are not able to bear moral burdens. One who condones moral oppression tightens a noose over his or her own humanity. To rebel against moral exploitation is a basic duty of conscience. Obviously, it is also crucial that the means of carrying on this rebellion not be contrary to conscience.

A mutiny of conscience against the moral exploitation of work brings to the forefront the question of human dignity. The question of dignity comes before the questions of work and compensation. Human dignity does not imply pride and empty ambition. One who thinks so does not understand human beings. Since treachery has occurred, fidelity must follow. Since humiliation has been inflicted, respect must ensue. Since there was degradation, equality must come. Dialogue is possible only when there is a common grammar. Ethics are the grammar of relationships between people, and their principle, human dignity.

It is for this reason that our present defiance is not an ordinary mutiny. Rather, it is a voice—great and piercing—calling the people to fidelity.

ILLUSION

Today, more than ever before, cognition and knowledge have become integral parts of work. This means that before a human being begins to shape raw materials, that human being must make an effort at a comprehensive cognition. Cognition precedes the action and constantly accompanies the action. An error in cognition can result in catastrophe for the work. Today, every worker is, at a certain stage of work, a scientist of sorts. In other words, everyone must pose a question about truth. I wish to build a bridge, but can I do this without taking cognizance of the true width of the river, the depth of the water, the height of the flood tide? As technology progresses, the role of science in work increases all the more. This process not only cannot be stopped but should not be stopped. Humans are intelligent beings; that is, they should act in the light of truth.

However, where there is cognition there is also the possibility of various illusions that deform our view of events and objects. As long as these illusions are not connected with work, they remain relatively harmless. Occasionally, however, they penetrate deeply into the reality of work. Then they occasion simply tragic results. For example, in medieval times autopsy was strictly forbidden,[13] since it was considered a profaning of the deceased. This illusion for a long time inhibited the progress of medicine. In India—a country where people are dying of starvation—"sacred cows" are untouchable and not to be eaten. Even today, in some circles, blood transfusion is considered to be a transfer of the soul from one person to another and is forbidden. There are religious, philosophical, ideological, and racial illusions; individual and social illusions. It is very difficult to fight illusions, even though they cause enormous harm. This fight is the duty of science since science, by its nature, strives for the truth.

Illusion in cognition—cognition that conditions work and accompanies it—occasionally produces results similar to those evoked by the exploitation of work. Illusion spreads over our view of the world and particularly over our view of people. From nowhere, people begin to feel hurt and oppressed. To them, people seem to be divided into exploiters and exploited. They believe that there is a concealed malevolence behind their suffering—the ill will of an individual or a group. However, closer examination of the situation confronts us with an astonishing paradox; there are the exploited, but there are no exploiters. We all, though each in a different way, are victims of illusion. We have misled ourselves because a shared superstition has duped us.

Let us consider one of several possible examples, an example that concerns the concept of common property and private property. Certain thinkers of the past considered the institution of private property to be the major source of social ills. Others thought the opposite, that is, that the very abolition of private property could become a cause of unhappiness. A controversy flared up that lasted decades and even centuries. In these disputes the concept of property played a key role. What does it mean that something is someone's property? What does it mean that something is common and something else is private? Unfortunately, these basic concepts have not been fully clarified. This lack of clarity was the reason that they became the nest for various illusions.

Let us consider two examples.

First, look at a red billiard ball. We say, "This ball is red." The word *is* underscores the close association between the redness and the ball. We say that the "redness is a *property* of the ball." The word *property* is used here in a radical sense—the same concrete redness cannot be the property of any other object. Only this ball "has" this concrete redness. This idea of property originates from metaphysical reasoning, which does not deal with life in society but is concerned with the internal structure of beings. Nevertheless, this kind of thinking has been transferred to other kinds of reasoning, for example, thinking about the relationship between someone as a proprietor and what that person possesses as proprietor. The consequence of such a transference is the radicalization of the idea of possession. It thus seems that a person "has" land, a forest, a tree in the same way that a ball "has" redness. What is mine cannot be yours, ours, common. The tree is mine; mine is also its fruit.

To eliminate the wrong that stemmed from this concept of property, certain thinkers proposed "abolishing" private ownership of all means of production. By doing this, they wished to destroy evil at its root. They wanted the fruit of a tree that serves life to be truly common, in order that no one lack that fruit. These thinkers did not see any other way than to accept that commonality begins right with the tree. A common tree must bear common fruit.

Ingenious ideas occasionally undergo less ingenious simplifications. This is how illusions are born. Illusion in our case consists in the belief that possession of trees in common is a sufficient guarantee of common fruit. The transformation into commonality was to arise from the very beginning—from the tree. It was necessary to proclaim with clear legality that after a given time trees would be common. Did common fruit result from this? Unfortunately, the tree proved to be masterless, "no one's tree." From a radical "I have" the road led to the no less radical "you do not have." The redness that ceased to be the property of a ball found itself in a vacuum. The tree, instead of bearing a great deal of common fruit, stopped bearing fruit entirely.

Why? Were not the original intentions good ones? Was not the purpose of all this to provide abundance for all? Certainly. But despite everyone's goodwill, somewhere an illusion crept in. It seems that the basic source of this illusion was a metaphysical style of thinking about life in society. All proposals for change were made within the framework of this style. In fact, this style must now be totally discarded. Ethics is the proper way of thinking about life in society. Metaphysics has other worries to attend to.

The second example is a beautiful example of common property, speech and language. Language is a condition and means of coming to understanding between people and for this reason can be called, in a proper sense, the "common property" of people. Language is a common property of people because the meaning of words used by people is held in common. This commonality is eminently expressed by the little word *for:* speech is for people, words of a language are for people; sentences and stories are constructed for people. The commonality here is thus primarily a commonality of fruit. What is truly common begins at the level of the fruit. The desire to use a common language causes us to try to adopt what is our own to the needs of the community. We "position" our lips and other vocal organs in such a way that they can participate in the commonality and can serve this commonality. A common fruit radiates backward and permeates what is personal and causes it—without ceasing to be someone's property—to serve the commonality.

In work—as in language—the primary objective is that the fruit be common. Bread should be bread for all. The more that fruit is fruit for all, the more common becomes the tree that grows the fruit. Common fruit radiates a spirit of commonality toward everything that contributes to its origin. A tree that serves all people by bringing a bounty of fruit, is under the control of everyone—even if it has a single proprietor. The commonality here has a moral, not a metaphysical, character. More important than the question "How is it?" is the question "Whom does it serve?" Land and trees that do not serve a human communion are not common. If, in spite of everything, we call them common, it means that we have fallen victims to some sort of illusion.

We have an amazing paradox before us—mistreatment without mistreating, spiritual oppression without an oppressor, disturbance of the rhythm of work without disturbance. We find ourselves helpless in a world that we do not understand. The simplest, most obvious things cannot be recognized by people. In this situation we must call to our aid a kind of thinking that is free of superstitions.

There is no illusion that does not have some truth hidden in it. We have an idea about common possession of the means that serve life. Around this idea many controversies and misunderstandings have grown up. Some have been for abolishing private property, others, against it. But the idea has not been given final elucidation. Meanwhile, there is truth as well as illusion in it.

The truth about common property is truth in an ethical sphere. "Common" is what is for me, for you, for us. The ethical essence of commonality is conveyed by the word *for*. Common is, above all, the fruit of work. Only subsequently and gradually the means that serve the production of this fruit come to be more or less common. The means are common only inasmuch as they serve this fruitfulness. One can substitute a metaphysical style of thinking for this ethical truth: Then, instead of thinking of fruits, one thinks of their cause. One devises new measures to make the causes of fruitfulness "common." It appears that only a "common" tree can give common fruit. With this, the idea of commonality somehow collapses—a bird that usually rests on the branches of the tree seeks to rest on its roots. That is the bird's illusion.

The role of thinking vis-à-vis illusion is twofold. Thinking is concerned with unmasking illusion and finding the element of truth within it. Since there is no illusion that does not have a speck of truth within it, science must rescue this truth. The point is that people who have gone through the trials of illusion should come out wiser and not more embittered.

SCIENCE

SCIENTIFIC work is also a person-to-person dialogue—a dialogue that aims to reach the truth. Scientific dialogue distinguishes itself in this, that its striving for truth is persistent and uncompromising. Truth and dialogue are the destiny of science. Science was born when human beings, prior to all their wondering about the universe and prior to their acting within the world, decided to put forth the question What really is it that exists or may exist? The answer to this question cannot be obtained in isolation; whoever learns something does so with others and always shares with others the fruits of cognition. The truth and the achieving of it cause people to enter into special relationships. It is necessary for us to become more familiar with these relationships. Even before this, however, comes the question What is truth?

We speak about truth in at least three different contexts. Most often we speak about true cognition—cognition is true when it is consistent with the reality to which it refers. I assert that it is snowing today, and in reality it is as I maintain. We also speak about a true or false expression of our convictions. Speech is true when it is consistent with the convictions of the one who speaks; otherwise speech is a lie. Recently, there has been much talk about "existential truth," about the "truth of being." One "is in truth" when in each situation—good or bad—one is able to be oneself. We say that such a person is an "authentic" person. In all three instances, the truth uncovers its fundamental, ethical dimension—it is the source of moral commitment for human beings. A scientist perceives this commitment more strongly than other people. Scientists are people who cannot lie in any situation—they can lie neither through their evaluation of things nor through the expression of their convictions nor through their attitude.

Engaging in science, one is engaged in a multilateral dialogue with other people. Two planes of this dialogue seem to be essential—one of them is defined by the little word *for* and the other by the little word *with*. One engages in scientific pursuits *for* someone and *with* someone—"with someone" and "for someone." The person *with* whom we engage in science is always to some degree our master, the one *for* whom we engage in science is a pupil and recipient of the truth—someone who is more interested in the fruits of science than in the way they are obtained. In modern times the problem of science has become immensely complicated. Science is expensive, requires good organization, and often must fulfill ideological or even political aims. For this reason, to the two planes of human meetings listed we must add a third—the relationship with the "organizer" of scientific life. The organizer is neither a master nor a pupil but influences the life of science by deciding about its organization, its material resources, and sometimes even about the ultimate goals of its investigations. Science needs the organizers, even though this need is associated with certain dangers for science.

Let us turn our attention to the ethics of science from the point of view of "with whom" and "for whom" is science. Let us focus our attention especially on the danger that emerges from the activity of the organizer of science. Let us pose a key question: In what does the exploitation of science consist, especially from the side of its organizers? By posing this question, we do not exclude the possibility of exploitation of science on the other planes of scientific dialogue. However, the problem of the organizer appears to be more relevant and yet more difficult to grasp.

The first form of disruption of the dialogue of scientific work is the "error of the master." The essence of this error is that a co-worker is not introduced by the "master" into the mainstream of current scientific development and thus must remain somewhere at its periphery. The questions posed by such a master are not the proper questions for a given science, are untimely and out of place; the methods employed do not fit the problems; the answers advanced are not relevant to the actual investigations. The scientific work is wasted. In the final analysis the master betrays the pupil; a worker, a co-worker; a researcher, another researcher—their paths must separate. Only the bitter taste of unfulfilled hopes remains.

It happens that an organizer usurps by personal prerogative the role of the master. The organizer has in hand forces that are outside of science, the promise of honors, the threat of withholding positions and facilities; the organizer controls the money needed for science and for the scientist's upkeep. For certain reasons, the organizer is not satisfied with the external administration of science but also craves for internal control. Most frequently, the organizer's purpose is to subjugate the science to the authority of an ideology that the organizer represents. To achieve their aims inconspicuously, organizers may assume the posture of a "master," but they act more through sheer force than by the power of persuasion. They start to impose on a science their own methods, dictate its questions and answers, define the direction of its applications. What do they gain from all this? They achieve not only a great influence on science but, above all, an illusion that their ideology and their activity are consistent with the laws of science. "Organizers" exploit the authority of science to justify their own actions in the world.

The moral exploitation of science here takes the form of "oppression of science." Science somehow "suffocates" in the overconfined space. This is perceived especially acutely by scientists themselves. Their goodwill to serve the truth failed to find corresponding goodwill in their environment. In the world of scientists, the wall of misunderstanding rises. Instead of dialogue with the leaders of science, we have a dialogue with epigones and eventually only a sad monologue somewhere on the fringes of the struggle for the truth. Even if in this monologue there are some discoveries, they are not the discoveries that are the primary aim of the commonwealth of scientists—they are not timely discoveries.

The fundamental property of scientific truth is its universal-ity—scientific truth is the truth for everyone. This is so because science concerns itself with basic truths; basic truths are the same for all people. Science does not investigate the individual secrets of the heart, unless such secrets are somehow associated with general affairs (e.g., the science of history). It is said appropriately that science is the property of all, that science is for everyone. The universality of science expresses itself by the word *for.*

A second disturbance of the dialogue of scientific work is the "error of the pupil"—an error in the reception of the fruits of scientific work. This error consists in a selective approach to the fruits of science, that is, keeping some of them and spurning others. Often in doing so one changes the sense of the conclu-sions—one makes axioms out of conjectures, final theories out of hypotheses. One also claims that science has definitively solved certain problems, though in reality no such thing has taken place. The pupil becomes an enthusiast, the enthusiast, a believer. The pupil either drinks from the chalice of science everything but scientific criticism or drinks only criticism but leaves out the truth. In this way pupils on their own sidetrack themselves from the development of science.

Organizers are also recipients of the fruits of science. It may happen that it is they who want science to produce the results that confirm their ideology and their authority. Organizers make themselves "proprietors" of scientific truth; they buy it the same way that one buys hats. True, they do not directly influence the production of hats but choose selectively from ones already made. They themselves make decisions on technical applica-tions, on publication, on advertising. They seek only those theo-ries that justify their interest. Their enthusiasm for the fruits of science is defined a priori.

Here too we are dealing with the moral exploitation of scien-tists. This exploitation assumes the form of an "abuse of sci-ence." Abuse, as we know, is the corrupt use of something inher-ently good. It starts with a falsification of the original picture of the fruits of science. One takes only a part and assigns to this part an absolute character. Out of wonderful theories, one constructs the tools of death. What do scientists feel upon seeing such a fate for their fidelity to the truth? They feel one thing— they want to stop proclaiming truth. They would prefer to remain alone with this truth. This desire represents an extreme reaction to the realization that they are being exploited.

The oppression of science (error of the master) and abuse of science (error of the pupil) are the two most basic forms of moral exploitation of scientific work by those who participate in scientific dialogue either as pupils or as co-workers or as organizers of scientific life. The exploitation of science aims directly at the goodwill of scientists, since ultimately the exploitation is reduced to an accusation that the scientists have lied or participated in a crime. This is significant; the exploitation is not economic in nature. The issue is not that the scientists are underpaid but that in the end they are not permitted to be scientists.

Can scientists defend themselves against this exploitation? There is a single basic condition for the defense, internal faithfulness to the truth. The issue is not only that of being a scientist but of simply being a truthful person. One must first be a truthful person to be able to become a scientist. Internal fidelity to the truth is a value that neither fire nor worms destroy. Everything that is honest in science starts from fidelity, and every exploitation of science stops short of fidelity.

ART

THE WORK of an artist serves life differently than does the work of a farmer. Art reveals a deeper meaning of human life and gives to life new value. The work of the farmer serves life by sustaining it. We reach for a volume of poetry, not because we feel a hunger for it similar to that for bread, but because we want to see life in a different, higher light. Poetry is an art that is capable of "transforming bread eaters into angels" (J. Słowacki). Artistic creativity originates from freedom and inspiration. Freedom should not be equated with license. There is license when "everything is permitted" because there are no values at all. There is freedom when a person is given certain values from which to choose—discarding some and accepting and acting upon the others. Inspiration is like a light that illuminates that which should be chosen. Artistic creativity always chooses by the light of values—a choice that is followed by creation.

Without farmers, artists would not have bread. Without artists, the life of farmers would be a life of earth-bound robots. Full development of humanity requires the cooperation of both. Some believe that the evolution of human work is moving toward all human work being like the work of an artist—springing from freedom and inspiration. Perhaps this is true; then art would be the hope of a working person. One cannot speak about work without talking about artistic creativity—about art. Today, it is already known that at least one work of solidarity is the work of art—work among people, for people, and with people. This work is the art of dialogue. Later we shall say a little more about it, but in the meantime, let us limit ourselves to the artistic creativity of the artists of beauty.

There are some who believe that art is above ethics. No ethical principle would concern art since art transcends good and evil. They who think so do not know how much they wrong art. Artistic creativity and works of art are permeated by ethics. There are several factors responsible for this. Artistic creativity is, above all, free creativity, and freedom is the first condition of ethics. This creativity, moreover, is not licentious creativity but follows certain values—this is the second condition of ethics. All the values served by art can be reduced to three: beauty, truth, and goodness. Beauty is a fundamental element of art; the creativity of an artist is a creativity within the element of beauty. This does not mean that truth and goodness are excluded; indeed, it is always a concern that beauty when created be true beauty and good beauty. The Artists who sense this are already in the sphere of ethics—the most fundamental morality of creation. They know that they ought to choose in creativity, choose between beauty and nonbeauty, truth and untruth, goodness and nongoodness. A work of art is the fruit of a creative choice of values. Where else can one find a more obvious ethics?

No one has access to what happens in the soul of an artist at the moment when freedom and inspiration come to fruition through creation. Artists themselves are unable to speak about it. We see the fruit of the creation, but in this fruit there is enclosed an essential truth about creativity and its ethical dimension. The problem is that this truth is written in a unique way and that it cannot be translated into the language of universals. One who wants to know what statement of value a given piece of art makes about the work of an artist must simply look at it. Each creation has its ethos just as each artist has an individual sensitivity to values.

But we are supposed to write about the ethics of artistic creativity, that is, to transform the concrete into the universal. How shall this be done without falsifying the issue? I think the best way will be to take under consideration a particular example of a work of art and ask, What does this artwork tell me?

Here is a monument.[14] On three colossal crosses three anchors—symbols of hope—are nailed. Three crosses and anchors reign over the shipyard, over the city. At the foot of the crosses is a sculpture reminding us of events of former years and a fragment of a poem by Czesław Miłosz.[15]

> You, who have wronged a simple man
> Bursting into laughter at the crime
>
> . . . .
> Do not feel safe. The poet remembers.
> You can slay one, but another is born.
> The words are written down, the deed, the date.*

---

*Translation from the Polish original kindly provided by Richard Lourie.

In this monument, there is *truth*. First, there is the truth of recollection. Ten years ago the first workers of this shipyard perished here. Looking at the monument, we think about that tragedy: "The poet remembers." The work of art does not allow us to forget. The monument fixes that event, protects it from passing away, protects it from the eroding work of time. But this is only one motif, only the first raising of the curtain. Immediately after it, or even with it, comes the second, deeper one. The point is not only not to forget but also to see something new, something invisible to the naked eye.

Three crosses and the crucified anchors. The anchor is here as a twofold symbol—a sign of work and a sign of hope. We know that the work of people of the sea is particularly associated with the anchor. Thus, the anchor is associated with what was crucified here—work and hope. Many people die every day throughout the world, but those people who perished here perished through their work. A human being may die in many ways— those who heard those shots experienced how hope dies in the heart. This work of art shows us the essence of that tragedy—a blow that remains a blow to the work and hope of all humankind.

Yet there is also a cross. This is likewise a reminder. This cross is a replica of the Cross of Golgotha.[16] There too Hope was crucified. But was it killed? Did not Hope resurrect itself? We read, "The poet remembers. You can slay one but another is born."

A work of art takes us by the hand and leads us to what is deeply hidden, leads us to essential truth. It shows us this truth; it shows this truth through itself. There is no other way to show it. It shows truth by a great condensation, a wonderful synthesis. One can stay a long time, read and think, understand and contemplate.

In this monument, there is also goodness. I mean ethical goodness, that is, a testimony to human goodness. The monument tells about a past tragedy in such a way as to prevent such a tragedy repeating itself. Art threatens, warns, and summons to fidelity. Once again the ancient commandment of God "Thou shalt not kill" becomes a concrete and pointed commandment: Do not kill work, do not kill hope. "You, who have wronged a simple man, bursting into laughter at the crime, do not feel safe."

Is that all? There are three crosses. On Golgotha there were also three crosses. From one of them a voice cried, "Forgive them; for they know not what they do" (Luke 23:34). From another cross the voice was similar. Yet from still another cross, blasphemies poured out. Which cross shall be our cross? We have to choose. But no, here each cross is the same. On each cross is the same Hope. And the voice must be the same. The cross has been chosen! We must make it our own cross.

A work of art beams a message.

The call of great art is often a protest. But the protest of art is never a nihilistic protest. Each true "no" of art is born from art's "yes." Art gives a testimony of human greatness—greatness that builds itself up even in tragedy. A new solidarity of consciences among people is going to continue to be a seal of this greatness.

A work of art speaks just as conscience speaks to conscience.

Beauty—sometimes called *form*—is like a light that emanates from a work of art. The beauty radiates, making a unique synthesis of truth and goodness. Beauty focuses our glance, directs our attention, gives us something to see and to think about. The essence of beauty is to uncover and to give promise of discovery. Beauty unveils truth, and that truth is a truth about goodness. A work of art is a synthesis of these three values. It speaks—speaks through itself.

We know that the work of an artist does not always bear the fruits of such harmony. When harmony is lacking in the work of art, we say that the work is false, not authentic. The beauty in it is an empty beauty. The truth is only an illusion of truth. What it calls for is also an illusion of goodness.

Spurious works of art may have two sources, the artist's lack of ability, or external oppression. Ethics has nothing against untalented artists—they have the desire but not the capacity. We absolve them willingly. Ethics, however, cannot allow creation under duress, without freedom of choice and without inspiration—

that is, nonauthentic creativity. When, in spite of these conditions, an artist decides to create, ethics suspects a moral exploitation of the artist's work. This exploitation prevents the artist from being authentic. What is created is empty. The work of art pretends to be something that it is not. By this, it betrays the fall of a human being.

DEMOCRACY

DEMOCRACY literally means "popular rule," "the rule of the people." Those governed are at the same time those who govern. What does "the rule of the people" mean? Why should "the rule of the people" be, according to some, so very much recommended? The answer centers around two positions. Some say it is because the people are the bearers of "truth," because the people are always right. Others say it is because the people are the most numerous and, therefore, have the greatest power.

The people are always right, are bearers of truth. This idea means that those who are at the bottom of the social ladder know best what are the good and bad sides of the system in which they are living. Do you wish to know what our social system truly is? Then do not ask sociologists, do not ask governors, party secretaries; ask workers, ask farmers. Their knowledge of the system does not come to them secondhand—from reading newspapers and books, from stories told by acquaintances—but is inscribed on their backs by harsh daily reality. Those who are at the top have, perhaps, a broader view, but of real life they know only what "apears" to them. They do not take

part in the daily struggle for bread. This is why the absolute truth
is found among the people. From here grows democracy—the
rule of the people's truth.

People—say others—are the masses; objectively speaking they
are an invincible power. History rolls on in the direction determined by mass movements. History does not know the concepts
of truth and falsehood, goodness and evil; it knows only the
concept of power. Whoever is stronger holds the cards of the
future. Therefore, in every concrete event, it is imperative to
gauge precisely the will of the majority and then to work consis-
tently for its realization. Ways of establishing the wishes of the
majority may be different, but each of them is proper provided
that it leads to the actual establishment of that will. Democracy
is born from ascertaining the wishes of the majority. What is this
democracy? It is the rule of the people's power.

There are also attempts to find the golden mean between these
two extremes. One then speaks about "democracy of the nobility," "democracy of the bourgeoisie," "democracy of the proletariat." One tries to fuse into one those who possess truth with
those who have power at their disposal. And so, for example, the
proponents of proletarian democracy exclaim that the proletariat
fuses within itself both truth and power. The proletariat contains
in its self-knowledge the truth about life in society because the
proletariat carries the greatest burden of this life. The proletariat's truth about the social system is equivalent to the pain of its
work. The proletariat also has the greatest power, since it holds
in its hands the key to modern industrial production. By fusing
in itself both truth and power, the proletariat is the most progressive social force. "The instinct of the working class is infallible."
Therefore, proletarian democracy is an expression of both truth
and power. Something quite similar was said in the past about
the nobility, the peasantry, and the bourgeoisie, simultaneously
praising their corresponding "democracies."

The problem of democracy, as can be seen, is complex. With
no great effort, we can discover that the two extreme positions
on the idea of democracy are absurd. Those at the bottom of the

social ladder certainly know the dark sides of the system, but they do not see the origin of these dark sides nor how to get rid of them. Most often, they fall into the trap of the illusion that some "bad people" rule their world. Those at the top rather easily and quickly disassociate themselves from the masses and, while surveying their horizons, ignore the power and plight of masses. Here, without doubt, is a paradox: Hitler was elected democratically, whereas Pope John XXIII[17] (and the other popes) were elected in a way that clearly departs from the ideal of classic democracy.

Is there a way out of this impasse?

I am developing here the thesis, perhaps a risky one but nevertheless one that seems correct to me, that, above all, ideas are democratic and that the social forces that carry and represent these ideas are so only secondarily. Masses without ideas are blind, whereas an idea without the support of the masses is powerless. The majority is not always right. Nor is power always on the side of the majority. The democratic character of a given social movement is decided by an idea that manages to gather around itself the energy and hearts of many. There are ideas that are dear to everyone, and there are other ideas that are dear to only a few. The former are democratic by nature, the others are by nature nondemocratic. There is no point in trying to change this. For one thing, there is no point in presenting nondemocratic ideas as democratic and, obviously, vice versa.

What does it mean that a certain idea is democratic? Two aspects of such an idea require particular emphasis—rationality and freedom. To become democratic an idea must be rational and must lead toward liberation.

An idea is a rational one when it forms the basis for social order. Social order is formed by assigning to each person a certain function in the context of other people, and as a result, each becomes useful to others. In exchange for carrying out a function useful to others, one receives from others the means to satisfy one's own needs. The teacher who does not farm receives bread from the farmer who, in turn, does not teach reading and writing. Rationality means harmony between social functions and their bearers. Where there is wisdom, there is also clarity. Clarity makes it possible to understand life. With the smallest effort, we can obtain a relatively large gain.

Usually the rationality of a system is not obvious at first sight. It is only when order collapses that somewhere a cry rises to return to reason. When there is bread, people do not care about agriculture; when there is a shortage of bread, everyone asks what happened. Then the slogan "More bread!" becomes democratic. Everyone who has a brain and a stomach—without persuasion and propaganda—declares himself behind the slogan. Democratic communion is born spontaneously. Only the paranoiac can claim that such a communion has been inspired by antisocial forces.

In short, an idea is democratic to the degree—obvious to anyone who can think—that it determines the need to realize values indispensable for the life and survival of people and their communion.

A democratic idea has still another aspect; it must delineate a person's scope of freedom. Not everything must be organized. Not everything can be organized. A human being must have some area of freedom and liberty. The concept of humanity is also the personal and spontaneous creation of an individual. The richness of a person is expressed through freedom, a richness that should not be limited by any assigned function. Human beings are the artists of their own lives and shape them according to their own perceptions of happiness and honor. Freedom is always associated with some degree of unpredictability.

Freedom is indispensable and freedom is disturbing. Without freedom, no deed, no desire, no accomplished function, will be a person's own deed. People in their deeds ought to be themselves. Where freedom is lacking, people are not themselves, even when they do what is required of them. But people may be themselves (feel that they are themselves) in something that is wrong. This is the source of the apprehensiveness associated with freedom.

The second feature of the democratic idea is its association with freedom. An idea is democratic when it delineates for the largest number of people the greatest possible sphere of individual freedom and responsibility, simply, when it enables everyone to be himself in his life.

Rationality and freedom are opposites. The more there is freedom, the less things can be predicted. The more there is rationality the more things are regulated a priori. To join the ideas of rationality and freedom one must come up with something else—a third idea to unify these opposites. At each stage of history, there is a need for an idea that could represent a synthesis of rationality and freedom. Such an idea would be the expression of concrete democracy. Behind this idea the majority could declare itself. In the past, independence was such an idea in this country. Do we have such an idea today?

It seems so. The idea of human dignity has become an idea of "concrete democracy." Everyone feels this idea in one's own way, but the idea is basically held in common. The obviousness of human dignity expresses itself in the saying "They can starve us, but they may not dishonor us." Freedom expresses itself thus, "Let us be ourselves." Today, everybody finds within himself a sense of dignity, workers, farmers, intellectuals, and scientists. The idea of dignity is the background for all concrete hopes. Even in the call for bread, there is a call for the recognition of dignity. This is why today dignity is our democratic idea.

Human dignity outlines the ethical perspectives of human development. It speaks of the need for a social system that would provide the possibility for human development starting from within. What is external should take its beginning from what is internal. Our concrete democracy then is not—as some suspect—a "bourgeois" democracy. It is simply an ethical democracy being asked for in a unique way by the proletariat. The amazing force with which this democracy argues its case arises from ethics.

––––––––––

SOCIALISM

We have to bring out into the open the ethical content of the idea of socialism—an idea that has multiple meanings today. Socialism, before it became a theory of social development, was an ethical proposition valid to those who were aware of the fate of others, especially the fate of working people. Even today, at a time of social conflict, this ethical content pushes aside one or another social theory—economic theory, the theory of power, the theory of revolution—to bring into full view the common moral imperatives. These imperatives have primary significance in rejecting or accepting a specific socialist doctrine.

Socialism has wanted and still wants to build a socioeconomic system in which—to speak in general terms, and to point first of all to ethical intent—the people's attitude toward the land and all its riches, especially those riches serving the development of life, would not be an attitude that places insurmountable obstacles in the way of taking a brotherly posture toward other people. The ethical intentions of socialism are briefly as follows: when someone has too much bread and others suffer hunger, understanding and love cannot prevail between them. Only when people finally find the proper attitude to the riches of the earth and succeed in a just division of bread will all the causes for conflict and war disappear. Thus, socialism is interested in the creation of objective conditions of possibility for developing human brotherhood. First, we must decide our attitude to the riches of the earth; after that comes the time for love and understanding. Objective reality should take precedence over subjective reality since "being defines consciousness."

Several theses contribute to the theoretical—scientific—content of the idea of socialism. The first concerns the significance of work in human development. Human beings—so claim the socialist theories—become fully human in work and through work. Precisely for these reasons, every disorder and disruption of the work process proves to be a disruption of the process of human formation. The elemental form of the disruption of the process of work is exploitation of work; therefore, the struggle against exploitation is the primary human goal and is a form of struggle for true humanity. An "untrue" system of work generates an "untrue" people. This is one of the first theses of the theory. The others are as follows: The industrial proletariat plays a key role in building a true work system. The proletariat is the bearer of power and truth. It has in its hand all the means needed to bring about a social revolution, and only it knows best what social injustice means and how to liberate itself from it. What should the proletariat do? It should—here we come to the practical, political principles of socialism—bring about the expropriation of the means of production from the hands of private owners and make them common property. This is because the main source of exploitation is private ownership of the means of production (factories, mines, land, etc.).

This last point must be fully understood. Nationalization of the means of production is not an aim in itself. Nationalization of mines is carried out, not so much to give people the satisfaction that they are co-owners of the mines, but to provide them with a sufficient quantity of coal during the winter. The basic idea is simple; we nationalize the means of production in the way and to the extent required for common social use of the fruits of production. We do not nationalize the pens of writers and the brushes of painters, since the fruits of their work are in any case "for everyone." The aim of nationalization is to satisfy needs. When an aim is unreachable, a wise man stops shooting for it.

Socialism is not a monolithic current. One can distinguish in it at least two counterposed concepts, open socialism and closed socialism. The representatives of open socialism believe that their theory lends itself to modifications depending on changing circumstances. One can learn a great deal about socialism from the actual process of putting it into practice. Representatives of closed socialism assume that the theory of socialism is virtually complete, and nothing else is left except to bring it progressively into practice. Experiences derived from the process of building socialism do not bring anything essential into the theory. At most, they provide merely an external supplement.

To understand better the difference between closed and open socialism, let us briefly examine controversies that occur between the two. Since we cannot go into detail, we shall touch upon only one concept—the concept of exploitation of work. The issue of strikes and the right to strike are closely connected with the concept of exploitation. The concept of exploitation of work is the key to the idea of socialism. Having this key in our hands, we shall understand better the sense of this ideological current—socialism—that is so significant in our lives. The crux of the matter is that closed socialism has a concept of exploitation and of strikes that is different from that of open socialism.

It has been said that the task of socialism as a social movement is to abolish the exploitation of work. This is achieved by abolishing private ownership of the means of production. However, the question arises, after the abolition of private ownership of the means of production, does all exploitation of work disappear? Or, do only certain forms of it disappear? The answer to this question depends on one's theory of exploitation and on one's definition of it. One can define exploitation in such a way that an affirmative answer will follow; that is, after abolishing private ownership of the means of production, there is no more exploitation. With another definition of exploitation, the answer may be different; for example, only certain of its forms will disappear, while others will still remain. Closed socialism leans toward the first answer, and open socialism tends to favor the second.

Let us imagine that now, after the abolition of private ownership of the means of production, a group of workers comes to the conclusion that they are still victims of exploitation. People are conscious of being exploited. This means, as I have explained earlier (see "Exploitation" and "Suffering") that the working people suffer in work and through work due to the wrongdoing of another person (for example, a manager) and not through the natural resistance of raw materials. These people also believe that their suffering is needless and easy to remove. In spite of this belief, the suffering is not going away. What does such a consciousness of exploitation mean for open socialism and for closed socialism?

For open socialism, the awareness of exploitation constitutes an additional incentive to expand the currently accepted theory of exploitation. The idea is entertained that there may be various forms of exploitation. Abolishing its most obvious and most brutal form does not solve the problem once and for all. One must be always on guard. Socialism is, above all, this awareness. Thus, when a group of workers is convinced that they are falling victim to exploitation, the new task of expanding the theory arises. For closed socialism the issue presents itself quite differently. It admits to the possibility of only one form of exploitation—that resulting from private ownership of the means of production. So when the workers, now, after the abolition of private ownership, conclude that they are still exploited, this means, according to closed socialism, that they have fallen victim to some kind of delusion, some illusion; their consciousness does not reflect correctly objective reality. This poses nothing new for the theory. Additional tasks are presented only to the propaganda apparatus.

The issue of strikes—the right to strike—is closely related to the issue of exploitation. A strike is, as we know, the workers' voluntary refraining from socially necessary, or at least useful, work. The strike is a basic weapon of a worker against exploitation. In a capitalistic system, the strike is something natural and understandable. Workers who are not owners of the means of production "feel alienated" from their work, and this creates the possibility of a strike. But what is the situation after private ownership is abolished?

Closed socialism rules out the possibility of a strike after abolition of the private ownership of the means of production. Now, the workers themselves are the owners of factories. Can one strike against oneself? Since there is no longer exploitation, how can there be a strike? The motive for a strike under these circumstances can only be an illusory sense of exploitation.

Open socialism sees the issue differently. The rationale for a strike may be different depending on the actual circumstances. The abolishing of private ownership of the means of production creates the objective conditions for abolishing only some—the most cruel—forms of the exploitation of work. The abolition does not preclude other, less obvious variants of exploitation. A strike is not excluded a priori. Workers may protest against various forms of the "abuse of work"—for example, against being deprived of the fruit of their own work. What good does it do for workers to be co-owners of a coal mine if they cannot own a pail of coal? Such a protest does not have to mean that they feel alienated from their work; it may reflect a desire to be fully masters of the means of production. If socialism is subject to a developmental process, one can imagine a strike in the name of speeding up this process of development at a particular stage. This is the way open socialism sees the issue.

We have, then, two contrasting interpretations of the same phenomenon. For some, the awareness of exploitation is just an illusion; for others, it constitutes an expression of objective reality. For some, a strike is something essentially unacceptable; for others, it is something possible and even desirable—(obviously, only under certain conditions). This conflict between open and closed socialism is a part of our history. Naturally, none of us has to get involved in this conflict if one does not feel competent. Everyone, however, must understand it. Otherwise, we cannot comprehend our daily reality.

At this point one more question arises. We have spoken about the socialist ethos—What is its relationship to the Christian ethos? What is the relationship of the ethical inspiration of socialism to the ethical inspiration of Christianity? Through these questions, we reach to the very roots of the doctrine.

One must say that there is profound difference, but there is no contradiction. What does it mean to say that there is no contradiction? It means we are dealing, not with one ethos, but with two different ones—however, it is not that one proclaims "evil" what the other calls "good." One should not confuse the difference between something ethical and something unethical with the difference between something ethical in one way and something ethical in another way. Not every difference must be contradiction.

Socialism suggests that one should begin by ordering the relationship of human beings to the riches of this earth, since objective reality precedes what is subjective. To be concrete, one must first abolish private ownership and introduce a just division of material goods. This end is achieved by conflict and struggle against the owners of the riches. Christianity proclaims that one should begin differently; one must start by putting in order the relationship of one human being to another, by introducing the harmony of love. Subjective reality comes before what is objective. Justice is a fruit of love. If I fail to reach an agreement with another person, I shall fall into the age-old "an eye for an eye, a tooth for a tooth" (Matt. 5:38), and my purported justice may turn out to be a fruit of my cruelty. A proper relationship to the material things of this world is a projection derived from a proper relationship to another human being. If the sense "we people" disappears, then the sense that something is "ours" disappears also. It is easy to enter the road of struggle and revolution, but how do we exit from it? As we have seen, the approaches are different. Different approaches open the possibility of mutual enrichment. Out of the difference comes also a common element; both want to make people happy. This is paradoxical; how does it happen that, so far, the meeting of this one ethos with the other, both aimed at human happiness, has so often brought to humanity more sadness than happiness? Which ethos has been betrayed, and by whom?

REVOLUTION

THE IDEA of revolution is sensible only if one assumes that there is progress to life in society. In contrast, if one assumes that the history of humanity is an endless repetition of the same events, the concept of revolution loses its meaning and becomes replaced by the notion of coup d'état. Thus, one should understand revolution to be a social change that is a leap forward on the road of progress. One of the first theoreticians of revolution, G. W. Hegel,[18] wrote: "Changes in nature, although so infinitely variable, form a circular pathway that is eternally repeated. In nature, nothing truly new under the sun happens [Eccles. 1:9], and the multifaceted play of nature's forms brings only boredom. Newness is brought about only by changes that take place in the world of spirit." Let us remember, revolution is an event in the world of spirit. As the result of the conflicts and struggle between opposing forces, a new, spiritual power comes to be heard. Only where spirit rules can there arise something that has not existed before.

When we think of revolution, we ordinarily think of changing authority. This is not the happiest association, but let us stay with it for a while. So, a struggle between authority and its subjects takes place. The authority falls and the subjects assume power. Is this the end of it? If it were, then every coup would have to be called a revolution. The crux of the matter is not in the overthrow but in progress. To the factors of authority and subjugation a third factor must be added—progress. But what does this word mean? Is this not an exaggeration?

Let us consider the matter of revolution from different aspects. First, from the side of the subjects—Why do the subjects rebel? Then, from the side of progress—What is progress? In the third step, let us ask—Revolution, what is that?

Revolution is a matter of spirit but spirit living within flesh and bearing all the consequences of this incarnation. The basic consequence of corporal life is the need to satisfy hunger, thirst, and the need for shelter. When a person has nothing to eat, a pain grows within, and with the pain grows a sense of rebellion against those who have bread in excess. Yet, we know that one pain does not equal another. There is a profound difference between the pain inflicted by another person and the pain caused by resistant and mindless nature. There is no way to avoid natural pain; it is certain to arrive and to defeat us. But pain inflicted by another seems to be avoidable. People who inflict pain are responsible for it and, therefore, guilty of it. One can accuse them. One can tie their hands; one can punish them with death.

From that, the revolutionary consciousness is born. This consciousness reflects the rebellious feelings of one group of people against another. The aching needs of the body make themselves known through the defiance of consciousness. From the start, the suffering becomes imbued with spirit. The rebellious consciousness is a consciousness of the degradation of people's dignity. One person humiliates another. The pain of the humiliated one indicates that someone here is guilty. The sufferings of some are the offenses of others. Thus, the rebellion born out of this bears the seal of ethics. The hungry ones feel innocent; the guilt rests on those who are well fed. This is the source of a call for social justice; this call then becomes the driving force of history.

A revolutionary consciousness is not yet a revolution. It is only its potential firebrand. Moreover, the rebellion that arises from it may take the wrong path, the path of spurious ethics. Subsequently, an illusion of revolution occurs. The illusion lies in this, that to a just beginning there is attached an erroneous ethical principle—the principle of revenge. An eye for an eye, a tooth for a tooth—the revolutionaries assume the thrones of the tyrants; to protect their aims they take over the methods of the tyrants. In place of one dictatorship another is born. The principle of revenge works even further. A revolution devours its own children. A sea of blood must be spilled until the simple truth emerges—nothing can be built on rebellion alone.

All modern revolutions have been closely connected to scientific development and its technological advances. The word *technology* is burdened today with many not very savory connotations. One must, however, keep in mind those aspects that are basic and unchallengeable. Technology is the progress of human domination over nature. Development of science and technology led to a profound transformation of the tools of human work. When the tools of work changed, work changed and human beings found themselves in a new situation. Work became less demanding and more productive. At the same time work became totally socialized, dependent on collaboration with other people. This transformation in the sphere of work led to far-reaching social changes. New social classes were formed, as were new systems of governing. And—let us not forget—all this started in the laboratories of a few scientists who are responsible for the shape of modern science.

Nevertheless, technology is something still more. Its origin and development presupposes the worldwide dissemination of definite, rational knowledge. The old knowledge is no longer sufficient. One must learn to read and write; one must know the elements of physics, chemistry, economics, and so forth. Only through such knowledge can we feel at home in the world and rule, at least partially, over the world. One who understands, rules. Those who cannot understand must be swept away—even if protected by a host of soldiers. By becoming familiar with technology, the former slave can feel like the lord of the earth, but a king who does not grasp technology becomes a slave to superstitions.

The spirit of technology is not free of an ethical element. The pilot of a plane has a touch of the consciousness of a conqueror. Human beings achieve a new sense of dignity and power. They rule. They are no longer material for slaves.

From the progress of science and technology there emerges a ray of hope among the oppressed. There comes the possibility that there will be bread in abundance; it is only a matter of living more wisely, of organizing life in society more wisely. The dream of the rebels joins the wisdom of scientists. The point is not that revolution be a bloody revenge against tyrants but that it be a means of introducing wise order among people.

If tyrants must fall, it should not be simply because they were too bloody but rather because they were too stupid. Unhappy is the fate of those who do not "wise up" in time. This is the meaning of progress.

What, then, is revolution? Revolution is an event in the realm of the spirit. Revolutionary consciousness is not only a reflexive protest against harm done to one human being by another but also both a moral indictment of those who inflicted the harm and an acquittal of those wrongly harmed. It is also the hope that the contemporary progress of scientific and ethical thinking can bring a solution to problems that until now were impossible to resolve. Finally, here is a new conviction about the dignity of human beings who, because of the labor of their minds and hands, rule over nature. From this sense of dignity, there is but one step to assuming the responsibility for realizing the hopes of the oppressed.

True revolution takes place on the level of subjects and not on the level of authority. It is not important who rules but who are ruled.

The meaning of a revolution is seen in its fruits.

The first fruit is the disappearance of the former subjects. Each person has changed. In the new person there is no trace of the clay from which were formed the former slave, vassal, work force. People cannot, even if they want to, regain their former shape. They now have different bones.

The second fruit of revolution is the disappearance of the old authority. The king goes away because he is no longer needed. The progress in the technology of spinning did not depend on someone destroying the spinning wheel and thus forcing another person to invent the mechanical spindle but on the fact that for some time both devices were available and the spinning wheel showed itself to be obsolete.

A revolution, that is, an event in the spiritual sphere, is authentic to the degree that it is bloodless. The spirit rules through persuasion and not through fear. This is why a truly great revolution is, at the same time, a holiday of the liberation of a human being from the fear of other human beings.

RULING

Let us begin by differentiating between two types of social struggle, the struggle for bread and the struggle for power. The struggle for bread—from an ethical point of view—is a struggle for social justice. We have before us one more loaf of bread. How should we divide the bread so that there is enough for everyone? We live in a social grouping. Who is going to be the group's leader, and who are going to be the subjects? The struggle for power is sometimes called a struggle for "recognition"—recognition of power in someone. The struggle for bread has an economic character; the struggle for leadership has a political character. Different ideals dominate the two types of struggle. Social justice is the ideal of the first struggle. For the second struggle, the ideals are historically variable; in most recent times these ideals have been most commonly defined as a struggle for some form of social democracy. The two kinds of struggle often overlap. It is thus important to grasp the difference between them.

Let us first consider the struggle for the recognition of power as power. Such a recognition is always bilateral. If I recognize that someone is my ruler, I must accept that I myself am that ruler's subject. If I recognize that you are my master, I must accept that I am your slave. A man who recognized someone else as feudal lord made himself a vassal. The first recognition was a source of the social system known as slavery; the second recognition created feudalism. The act of recognition usually is not an open act made after reflection on the situation. Usually, we make it without reflection, simply by entering into social existence. The existence of this act of recognition and its meaning reveals itself only at the time of crisis, when the struggle for power reaches its highest tension. What happens at such a time?

At a moment of crisis, people demand justification for their recognition. Exactly why should they accept this and not another authority? The relationship of an individual to authority goes from the level of naiveté to the level of reflection. There arises a demand for "legitimization" of authority. The authority must show that there are rationales for its rule. The demand for legitimization of authority has a political—not an economic—character. Is such a demand something unusual? On the contrary, the issue is not only to determine whether an authority is truly an authority but to find out who I am as a member of a certain society. In asking about authority, I ask about myself. Politics appear here as an essential element of my self-knowledge. One may also say that if I want to understand myself I must find the answer to the following questions: To whom am I subject? To what degree? Why? This is a common right of a human being. At this point, the meaning of the concept of politics must be broadened. Political consciousness is not the privilege of a few but is an essential component of human self-knowledge, that is, the social existence of human beings. The relationship to ruling authority is like a stick with two ends.

Most often today we encounter two forms of legitimization of authority. Each has its strong and its weak sides. From this comes the possibility of criticism. The criticisms, however, must be different, depending on the kind of legitimization. Arguments to improve one system are not effective for another, and vice versa. (Aspirin is useful for the flu but does not help a fractured leg.) What forms can the legitimization of authority take?

Election of authority is the first form of legitimization. The general scheme is simple: Various candidates for a position of authority stand in front of the people. Each presents a program for governing. If there are doubts, the people pose questions, demand clarification and amplification. Thus, there are different programs, and behind them there are different people. On a certain day, voting takes place. The one whom the majority supports rules.

Here the act of recognition of authority has a particular character; it is a result of a more basic recognition, that the minority must defer to the will of the majority. Since such is the will of the majority, the minority does not resist it. This more basic recognition is not entirely obvious. Does the majority always want what is good? Does it want something beyond its own comfort? Can the majority not become misled by empty ambitions or promises without substance?

From this comes a need for political criticism and opposition. Criticism and opposition do not question the basis of the system; on the contrary, they confirm it and act within its framework. The proper recipient of the critique is the majority that voted for the authority. The opposition tries to convince people that it was right to question the elected authority. If the opposition succeeds, a different program and other people will earn the recognition of the majority in a new election. The process will then repeat itself; the new minority will assume a critical posture toward the new majority.

A social system of governance can be compared to a pyramid. The authority represents the peak of the pyramid. The base of the pyramid is formed by the majority of the subjects. The base of pyramid must always be broad enough so that the peak will not crumble. When a majority supports the peak, everything holds together somehow.

The second form of legitimization is a more or less direct recognition of the elite's leadership. Here, the general scheme is different. In a particular historical situation, it may happen that a certain social group has a great historic mission to play—for example, is capable of abolishing slavery. The majority is convinced that slavery cannot be abolished, but the elite knows that this is not so. It is as if history itself were placing the authority into someone's hands. The elite, at a certain moment, achieves political leadership. It proclaims its intentions, defines the means of their realization. But even an elite requires legitimization and must justify itself. How? In the most general terms— ideologically (occasionally legitimization may assume a religious character, e.g., in the Church). The recognition of authority is part of the recognition of the basic ideology of this particular authority. To be more exact, we recognize a given authority to the extent that its ideology finds justification in our experience or in our ideology. Naturally, one can accept the ideology either totally or partly, permanently or temporarily, but at this time, this is of less interest to us. What is important is the essence of the issue.

Ideological (also, religious) legitimization must always, at some point, call upon ethical experience. The historical mission being realized by the elite is in fact an ethical mission. In the example of the abolition of slavery, the basic condition is the widespread conviction that slavery is unworthy of humanity. Then, because of this obvious ethical principle, the elite, or a certain minority, may with a clear conscience rule the majority. An origin in ethics is the basis for the rule of an elite. This does not preclude other types of legitimization, for example, religious or economic, but these are not the most important types.

The relationship between authority and the people in this case cannot be represented, as before, by a pyramid. It is better illustrated by a picture of people on a trek; at the head of a marching column are the leaders, or the elite, and farther back, all the rest. The elite knows the promised land. The people know the intentions of the elite and have confidence in the elite. People recognize the leadership, and by doing so they recognize themselves as being led. But people cannot be unconscious of their fate. Therefore, the relationship between the people and the elite is a *reflective* one. The people reflect upon their own relation to the elite and the relation of the elite to them. Occasionally, the elite runs too quickly and disappears behind a bend in the road. Some-times the people, informed in advance about the issues, overtake the elite.

A reflective relationship between the people and the elite is based on shared ethical sensitivities. In the system of governing just described, ethics play a much greater role than in the system discussed earlier. This, however, does not mean that ethics are of no importance in the system considered earlier. There, the central point was the will of the majority; if the majority wants war, then there shall be war; if the majority wants legalized abortion, there will be legalized abortion. Here, it is different. Here, the authority is held accountable for its fidelity to the principles of ideology, ethics, religion. The basic norm is Do not betray! The elite cannot betray the people to whom it owes the fact that it is an elite to begin with. The people cannot deny their elite because the people would then become like sheep without a shepherd (Mark 6:34). The unity of the people and the elite is a unity of common ethics. One who damages this unity will be rejected by the people and denied by the elite.

I said at the beginning that the struggle for bread is something different from the struggle for power, that is, the struggle for recognition. This means that, while we are struggling for just bread, all the same we do not refuse to recognize the political authority that leads us. These are two different issues. Even when they go side by side, they are two different issues and not just one. When a village mayor turns out to be a thief, the strug-gle to replace him is not a coup d'état. One who does not see the difference here should consult a psychiatrist. Political critique has a twofold character, depending on the kind of recognition enjoyed by the authority. Either the criticism calls upon the ma-jority to change its opinion and to support those who are cur-rently in the minority, or it is the ethical reflection on the rela-tionship of the elite to the people and the people to the elite. These relationships are based, at least in part, on a common morality. Such a critique cannot be ignored. When I do not know who rules me, I do not know who I am. And it is my duty to know who I am.

The worry about bread has a different nature. One may say this is worry about the light around bread. One must have bread in the light to know how to divide it. This concern assumes that everyone has the right to bread. We hold the bread in a circle of light so that everyone may receive a just share. It is important to distinguish well between opposition and proposition. Opposition is associated with political self-knowledge and grows from a critical reflection on the question Why should I recognize a given authority? Proposition is a project of the just division of bread within the framework of the general political system. In struggling for just bread, I *propose.* I propose how to sow, so more will grow; how to divide, so all will share equally; who should divide, that the bread does not stick to the hands. The question of the village mayor John also concerns us from time to time, not as a mayor who rules, but as John who steals. John, when he stands near the bread, is a "functionary." What is a "functionary" supposed to do? He is supposed to "function." Thus, he is supposed to act according to the rules of the division of bread. "Changes of the personnel do not interest us." These changes are not the most important. We are only interested in the rules by which functionaries function and in the glow of light around the bread.

Having in mind this distinction we can say that the ethics of solidarity are the ethics of *proposition.* The ethics of opposition are of a different kind and order. One must remember this well to understand, among other things, the essential nature of the arguments about the corrupt village mayor that erupt among us from time to time.

TENDING THE LAND

AN OLD Polish word, *gospodarz,*[19] refers to an individual who has tied his fate to the land—to work on the land. With this term is associated the word *homestead.* A homestead is a tract that has been tamed by the work of the homesteader—homesteading. The meaning of all these words is deeply rooted in our history. Poland was primarily a nation of those who worked the land. Tending the land—the work of homesteader—is the oldest Polish work; Poland itself is the oldest homestead. One who delves deeper into history and looks behind the meaning of those words will find a common source for them in the ethos of people whose duty was the service of life. These people while serving life acquired something from the wisdom of life itself. Never in our tradition has homesteading on the land been considered an expression of concern exclusively for the homesteader's own interest. Those who did not understand this brought disgrace upon themselves. Working on the land has been an expression of service to others, and where there is service there is a vital sense of common rights. We are proud that our country, during the religious wars, was a land of tolerance. We could also be proud, I believe, that in our country famine was not a massive and persistent plague accompanying the course of our history. Famine was something exceptional, caused by the caprices of nature, not by human selfishness.

The concerns of a homesteader are not only worries about the land but also about the entire homestead, especially about the home. The dwelling is the heart and mind of the homestead. This heart and this mind have their history too. At the times of the partitions,[20] the threshold of the home on the homestead was a "stronghold" that defended the living national treasures embodied in the people. "Each threshold shall be a bastion to us." [21] The home became an "outpost" [22] in which each farmer defended self-identity. The one who deserted a homestead also committed an act of betrayal. But one is not betraying stones, trees, or soil as soil. When someone betrays, someone else is betrayed—a human being. Stones, trees, soil, and everything that makes up a homestead represented to the people a single, great symbol to which one must always remain faithful. To live in the heart of the communion of people one needs, above all, this one thing—wise tending of the land.

Today, we must understand better the nature of the bonds that bind the homesteader to the homestead. We must consider correctly the nature of the work of the homesteader. There is always a danger that we may treat this work as if it were the work of an industrial entrepreneur. The two images of a homesteader and an industrial entrepreneur sometimes overlap today, and this results in the blaming of one person for the errors committed by someone else. An industrial entrepreneur is not a homesteader. When I say "industrial entrepreneur," I think of a nouveau riche who feels no profound spiritual values and covers up personal deficiencies with money. For such a person, land is only a "raw material" to be exploited, and the homestead is a "factory" for production that brings a tangible profit. Can there be a greater contradiction than that between working on a homestead and running an "industrial enterprise"? However, frequently one cannot see the differences. Because of that, it should not be a surprise that in fighting the one we will often hit the other. This is like a policeman who instead of arresting the arsonist, arrests the person who cries "Fire!"

What does it mean that land is neither raw material nor a factory but just land—part of a homestead? What does it mean that the homesteader tends land rather than simply "produces food"? The answer cannot be discovered if we examine the issue from the outside. From the outside everything appears similar. One must take a look from within, from the side of the spirit, from the side of ethos.

The acreage that constitutes a part of the homestead is land; it is neither a raw material to be exploited nor a factory to "produce grain." This is what we must understand in the first place.

Raw materials are in the land, but they are not the land itself. They are something that human beings have to dig out of the land and then process into products that fulfill the various natural and artificial needs of the people. Raw materials alone do not fulfill needs. Iron ore must become steel, and steel must become a car; crude oil must become gasoline; coal must find its way to the ovens and transform itself into heat. But what does it mean to process raw material? Unfortunately, it means to consume raw materials. After using the raw materials, an empty space is left behind. Can one do the same with the land? The land is not for "exploitation." The land must endure. One must deal with land in such a way that it remains land. For this reason, one has to say unequivocally, Land is not a raw material.

One cannot treat land as if it were a tool, that is, like a factory "producing food." The land does not "produce"; land truly gives birth. When we cultivate the land, we use tools, but the land itself is not a tool. A tool is an extension of our ability to act. As a tool is used, it wears out and ultimately is discarded. It is no longer needed. In contrast, the land by itself has the ability to bear the "fruits of the earth." It cannot be worn out. Each fall the land must bring forth a harvest. Human beings must help the land to bear better and more fruit, and thus to support life. The land will serve human beings only when human beings are able to serve the land. For this reason, the land that constituted the basis of a homestead we call *rola*[23] in Polish—precisely "rola,"—not a raw material, not a factory. This word has one more meaning—a role—that indicates the position the land occupies in the homestead. The land embodies in itself the work of generations. The power and might of land are the power of nature joined with the might of human work. Down through history, in the mystic potency of the soil, which has been land, there is a hidden memory—the memory of the land. The land is always "the land of forefathers." In the land is always some kind of heritage. We did not come here yesterday. It is not without significance that our land is the land of the Piasts.[24] In this land, the work of those past times still remains alive. The land comes from the work of others for others. It serves us because this was the desire of our forefathers. It will serve our children because such is our decision. The land is a meeting place—a place where the work of generations meet. Trees that grow from this land are always the trees of memory and hope.

In this connection, what does tending the land mean? When does a person become a caretaker of the land? One becomes a caretaker of the land when one's human cooperation with the land becomes an integral part of coexistence with other people. One has one's land from others and for others. I am the "proprietor" of my land, but here the concept of ownership has a unique sense. It does not mean at all that I can do with the land whatever I want. The homesteader's "to have" does not mean the same as the "to have" of the rich newcomer and the industrial entrepreneur.

Several times already, I have emphasized the analogy between work and speech. I said that work binds people in a manner similar to speech, that the fruit of work has a meaning similar to the meaning of the fruit of speech—the word. Let us reach once again for this example. The similarity, or rather kinship, between speech and work is particularly distinctive in the case of tending the land. One who tends the land "has" land in the same way as one "has" a word that one has just spoken. I say "tree." Is this my word? Yes, it is my word; it was formed in my mouth. Does this then mean that I am the "proprietor" of the word? Yes and no. Clearly, I did not invent the word *tree;* someone else invented it, passed it to others, thought out its pronunciation. The word is a part of a heritage. Do we possess words only for ourselves? Nonsense. Can one have a word for oneself alone? A word for oneself alone is only "mumbling," not speech. A word is mine, and at the very same time it is common; there is no contradiction in this.

Human work is like speech; the fruit of work—bread—is like a word, one's own and common. Here, individual ownership does not contradict commonality; commonality does not contradict private ownership. As there is more bread and bread is better, so speech can become more "common." The fact that the hands are "mine" and that the land is "mine," that the homestead is mine, does not contradict commonality. The only thing that contradicts commonality is land that lies fallow—fallow land is like a silent mouth, a mouth that utters no words. The homesteader's "to have" means "to give." The work of homesteading is true service.

Homesteaders work when they tend their homestead. This work is like a conversation between people. When they sow in the spring, they are speaking. When they harvest in the fall, they are speaking. When they take care of their orchard, they also speak. They speak with others, they speak to others. What they have becomes what they possess for others and from others. A spirit of commonality permeates this work from within. There is no need at all to impose a commonality from without.

Recently, certain new words have appeared in our language. These words deeply distort the picture of the work of the homesteader by suggesting that this work is like the work of an industrial entrepreneur who is concerned only with profit and exploitation. One says today, "private farm." This expression implies that to farmers, the land is like raw material or like a factory for the "production of food." Today, one also says, "individual farm." This would mean that farmers work there without a sense of commonality and with only their own interest in mind. Out of these conceptions a postulate is born for the "socialization" of the work of the farmers, a postulate to be put in practice by taking away their ownership of the land. The problem is not only in linguistic error. This language is the expression of a way of thinking. Thinking in which such concepts are possible is thinking based on an illusion—the illusion concerns the work of the farmer. One image is superimposed upon the other; as a result, we obtain a caricature. In this, the farmers' work is noticeably dissociated from history; there is an obvious demeaning of their role. Clearly, there are also embers of the moral exploitation of their work. Is there anything more contagious than thoughtlessness—thoughtlessness carried by meaningless words?

Can one "socialize" what of its essence is social? Can one "socialize" speech? In a certain sense one can, and in a certain sense, one cannot. Speech becomes very common when it is very intelligible to everyone. On the other hand, it does not become common through the fact of taking away from people their language and introducing a foreign or "common" one. The whole mystery of commonality is present in the little word *for.* This word is for others, but it is my language.

To "socialize" work on the land, one needs only one thing, to return to this work its own essence. This means, let farmers see for themselves how deeply they are rooted in the present communion, and let them work according to what they see. Our homesteads are of the Piasts. Our homes are outposts. Their thresholds have not ceased to be strongholds. We are not here just since today. We are not the first ones to use the scythe. We serve the land that serves us. Our work joins the work of past generations. By serving the land, we pick up the thread of our heritage and we create a hope for tomorrow. From here our dignity grows—the dignity of those who carry on the oldest Polish work. Our hearts are in the heart of mighty communion. I do not know which is more difficult, to plow fallow land or to rebuild the hearts of people worn by insults. Sometimes it is more difficult to rebuild the heart. However, the issue is not only to plow fallow land but also to protect from perishing those who tend the land. There is no farming without the heart for farming. The heart awakens for tending the land when one sees clearly into what heritage and into what communion one enters, when in the spring one goes to the field, faithful and laborious, wise and dignified, to sow the first seeds.

———

UPBRINGING

Upbringing and education are work with a human being and upon a human being—with a human being who is in the process of maturing. Upbringing and education create between mentor and pupil bonds that are analogous to those between parent and child. It is worthwhile to ponder this analogy for a while. Parenting can be perceived in diverse ways, some superficial and others more profound. When we look superficially, we see solely the fact that a parent is found at the beginning of a person's life but this person will develop and become progressively more distant from parents. One cannot remain a child during one's whole life. A son himself becomes a father. His coming to maturity then would occur at the point when he recognizes his distance from his father. However, if we look deeper we notice something different. Parenting is not merely passing on life; being a father also means passing on hope. The father is the trustee of the child's hope; he is the pillar and strength of this hope. We are the children of those into whose hands we have entrusted our hopes. What does it mean to be a child? It means to entrust to someone one's own hope. What does it mean to be a father? It means to become a trustee of someone's hope. Hope is the source of our life. For this reason one who brings hope to a person is that person's spiritual father.

When we reflect on the ethics of education, we enter the world of the hope of a maturing human being. We must put it this way: Only those who have hope truly educate and bring up others. One should also add that they educate by shaping the hope of those who are being educated. Education and upbringing are labor over the soul—labor according to hope. Only after hope does love come, does faith develop and an adequate sense of reality

take form. For this reason, the key principle of education and
upbringing is the principle of *fidelity.* Here, betrayal is not permitted—not permitted under any circumstances. One is not al-
lowed to tear apart the ties formed by entrusting hope. This
poses the threat of despair. The mentor senses it, and the disciple
knows it well.

Certainly, each of us has had some kind of mentor. What does
each of us owe to our mentor? I believe that I shall not miss the
truth if I say it is our awakening. At first, we traveled through life
not knowing what it was all about, as though we were half asleep.
The voice of our mentor jerked us from this slumber. The rest
had to be accomplished by ourselves. Socrates[25] compared the
work of a mentor to the efforts of a midwife, who helps a mother
during labor. Through the work of a mentor some kind of truth
is born in a person's soul. This truth becomes that person's
strength. The mentor does not create this truth; just as the midwife does not create the baby. The mentor only helps, by joining
efforts with the efforts of the one being helped. Nonetheless, this
help often appears indispensable—precious, as precious as a human being is.

The work of a mentor is primarily work on the hope of a
person. This is how this work is akin to parenting.

To understand this work better, let us look at it from another
side—from the side of its counterfeit. How many times have we
encountered counterfeit education? How many times have we
become stupefied by counterfeit mentors? Let us try to plumb
these experiences to capture in this roundabout way the essential
issues involved.

In working on human hope, a mentor can only try to shape
within the apprentice the apprentice's exclusive, personal, and
very own hope. What does this mean? We must remember that
in every person there are many different hopes. Some are shared
with other people; others are the exclusive, singular hopes of this
one person. One individual would like to be a poet, one, a saint,
another, a social reformer, still another, a revolutionary. Personal
and individual hopes emerge from national, professional, and

religious hopes. A human being lives primarily through personal hope. This hope, however, presupposes more common hopes. The poet must finish school; a saint ought to learn how to pray; a revolutionary should learn how to stand quietly in the lines in front of a food store.

Mentors commit a mistake when they concentrate only on the personal hope of an apprentice, as if it were a matter that depended on them. Such mentors want not only to arouse from slumber but also to lead by the hand those who have been awakened. They try to solve something that should be resolved only by the apprentice. The truth about hope is simple; one's personal hope must be found and made one's own by the apprentice alone. No one can order someone to be a poet, a saint, or a revolutionary. One can insist only on those things that are common: correct handwriting, prayer, decent behavior in a line. In the matters that are most personal and, therefore, most important for upbringing and education, the apprentice must have a sphere of free choice. Education presupposes freedom.

One who proceeds differently is erecting a house from the roof down. A mentor imagines that he is standing on the roof. After a while, he notices that only a few are listening to what he is saying. And yet, he speaks so beautifully! He speaks about such noble issues. If someone remains unmoved by those very lofty ideas, that person deserves nothing but scorn. In the soul of the mentor scorn for the pupils hatches. The mentor degrades his pupils, constantly treats them with reproach. Education and upbringing become a constant chastisement. The border line between mentor and prosecutor fades. The pupils do not find anything for themselves in the words of the mentor-accuser. The pupils know only one thing; the mentor is "dumping" on them.

From outside, however, everything seems to be in order. The pupils behave in the way expected of them by their mentors. They wear the proper uniforms, assemble for the roll call, submit to the ritual. The main effect of education and upbringing by imposition is that people move in circles in ritual order and do this with some degree of skill. The old truth confirms itself—the one who wants to accomplish too much does not accomplish anything.

The second danger for education goes together with the first danger. It is, however, much more serious. Its essence is *betrayal.* I have said earlier how great a role the experience of fidelity plays in the process of education and upbringing. The fate of a mentor and that of an apprentice are, to some degree, a common fate. When the children of Janusz Korczak's[26] orphanage went to the gas chambers, Korczak went with them. The planes of fidelity vary; and thus, planes of betrayal may also vary. It would be difficult to discuss here all the potential possibilities. There are open betrayals and there are hidden betrayals. When the betrayal is hidden, an illusion of fidelity is created. It is sometimes more difficult to accept the existence of an illusion of fidelity than to accept open betrayal. When the betrayal is open, there is no more suspicion, whereas illusion always provokes suspicion.

Fidelity emerges from the discovery of a simple fact: you and I, mentor and apprentice, are riding the same wagon. No one is standing on the roof. Our wagon is held in common. If the wagon falls apart, if our hope turns out to be a delusion, we all will be hurt. All, but . . . the faithful mentor knows that *his* tragedy must be greater. A faithful mentor is one who agrees to carry *this* burden on his shoulders. A mother nurtures when she speaks and when she is silent. When speaking, a mother gives orders, prohibitions, incentives; by being silent, she indicates that she is ready to sacrifice her life. Mentors must put themselves at risk. In a land of lies, their speaking of the truth must be louder than that of their pupils. In a land of injustice, their justice must be greater than the sense of justice of their pupils. In a land of hatred and suspicion, they must be more forthright and open. This is the essence of their *fidelity.* Those who entrust their hope to a mentor must know that the trustee is with them—together, which means that on the basic issues the mentor is a half pace ahead.

Where this "together" is lacking, an *illusion* of fidelity arises.

Pupils feel that they are repeatedly cheated. They are told of the need for honesty; but have mercy on them should they tell the truth to their mentor's face. Then, their mentor will remind them that besides truthfulness there is need for respect. Pupils sail in one boat and mentors in another. When pupils begin to sink, mentors give them good advice. This is supposed to express their "concern for the well-being" of their pupils. It happens after a time that their mentors advise them of only one thing: how to behave in order to drown painlessly.

Where does the illusion come from? It comes from the lack of distinction between what is primary and what is secondary, between what is the pupil's own and what is held in common. All along, one has been constructing the roof first. All along, one has been making choices for the apprentice. One has been dictating whether someone should or should not believe in God, without saying anything about the need for fidelity to the truth. One has been encouraging the struggle for world peace without being able to teach how to preserve peace within the family. One has been demanding sympathy for the poverty of Africans but has not been teaching how to see the fate of an overworked mother. Such an education, instead of sharpening a person's innate sense of reality, blunts it.

This phenomenon is accompanied by a significant change of roles. The role of the mentor is taken from the people's shoulders by the institutions. The institutions, instead of people, carry out the task of education and upbringing; people are, at best, a supplement to the institution. Everyone who enters the sphere of the institution is supposed to be affected by its magical action—everyone, the mentor as well. One and all believe that they should conform to the institution. In a green institution one wears green clothes; in a brown one, brown clothes. It is unimportant who you are; the only important thing is what you wear.

Against this background, the ethics of solidarity become the ethics of awakening—awakening to being a parent according to hope. One must go through the world of illusions toward what is basic. The basis here is fidelity. Those who have once accepted hope that has been entrusted to them, let them bear it throughout their whole life.

———

PERSUASION

Let us imagine a preacher who tries to convince his congregation that stealing is always ethically wrong and a sin. Toward this end, he chooses excellent arguments, quotes the opinions of the sages and verses of sacred scriptures. The sermon is flawless. There is only one problem: there is no thief among his listeners, and no one has an opinion contrary to his. In the final analysis, the sermon is not needed. So much effort for nothing! The listeners even feel slightly offended. They think to themselves, Who does he take us for?

The ability to govern people is, above all, the ability to persuade. To govern, one must argue for one's program; to argue, one must use one's brain; in using one's brain, one should know the people with whom one is dealing. Persuasion is the product of wisdom, but it is not wisdom to fail to be sensitive to values. The wisdom of persuasion calls upon feelings, memories, and hopes—open and hidden dreams—it calls upon a hierarchy of values. Today, in the age of television, we see that the external appearance of the persuader certainly also plays a role. A skinny person should not attempt to persuade others of the nutritional value of margarine; conversely, a fat person should not recommend to others the pleasures of an ascetic life. The appearance of a speaker should not contradict what the speaker is saying.

The essence of persuasion, however, is the vision of a person that every persuasion presupposes. This vision can sometimes be recognized after but a few sentences. From the style of persuasion, from the kind of arguments, from the assumed aims of the persuasion, it is easy enough to conclude what persuaders know about the people to whom they speak. This knowledge of theirs often decides the effectiveness of the persuasion. If the knowledge is honest and deep, if persuaders are open with people, we easily forgive them their slipups in language—and even some disorder in their argument. But if persuaders look at a person from the "position of a frog," they will not be helped by diction, argument, or the logic of evidence; everyone will automatically think, "Who do they think we are?"

Generally, we encounter two types of persuasion: persuasion aided by fear and persuasion aided by the promise of happiness. The first kind of persuasion is like cracking a whip over a horse—the horse is afraid and pulls the cart. The second kind of persuasion reminds one of placing hay in front of the horse's snout—the horse wants to eat the hay, stirs, and the wagon moves too. Therefore, to persuade means to frighten and to promise happiness. Let us consider this briefly.

One who persuades through fear assumes that the people are afraid and wish to avoid impending danger. However, not all fears are equal. There is the fear of a district court and the fear of the last judgment; there is the fear of losing bread and the fear of losing honor. With which fear can one human being frighten another? It would seem that those who use fear have free choice. There are so many fears in the world that something can be found for everyone. It would also seem that those who use fear will reach for the most common fear—to frighten the largest possible number of people—or the greatest fear. This, however, happens rather seldom. Most commonly, their imagination suggests to them their own fear. People persuading through fear most often use the fear that they are afraid of. In this way—perhaps subconsciously—they want to infect others with their own disease.

What is the reaction of the one who is being frightened? It is, without doubt, occasionally some kind of acquiescence. A dog that is being frightened will back off for a moment. But acquiescence has its limits. At some point the dog feels that it has nothing to lose and that its canine honor has been insulted. Then, the dog itself begins to frighten the one who frightened it. Who will frighten whom more? Who will frighten whom sooner? A duel of fears goes on. Usually, the winner is not the one who is frightened first but the one who intimidates the other more decisively.

Between acquiescence and resistance there is an intermediate road. This road leads toward understanding. The one being frightened dares to reflect. With what and why are they frightening me? Shortly thereafter, one goes a step further; they are frightening me because they are afraid themselves. This suspicion puts the frightened one on the same level with the one who frightens. It is not so bad—the one who frightens also has weaknesses. And, then there is a decisive step; since the frightener is afraid I must take the frightener *under my protection.* The roles are switched. Those being intimidated sympathize with those who are doing the frightening and take them gently under their protection. "Look, my little daughter, there is a wicked witch," says the mother. "Do not be afraid, Mommy, I will defend you," says the daughter. An odd situation emerges. The mother realizes that she does not know her own daughter. And all of this comes about because the initial concept of a person was erroneous.

The second form of persuasion is persuasion through the promise of happiness. The general formula is as follows: "If you do as I say, you will be happy." One can put this formula into action in a variety of ways; the happiness takes various forms, concrete and abstract, close and distant, universal and individual. Here also one may choose. In this case the character of the persuader reveals itself no less. One promises something that the other wants or that one has wanted.

There is a certain proportion between a condition and a promise. The harder the condition, the loftier should be the promise.

Truly hard and onerous work should always be "for the good of fatherland."

What is a person's reaction to a promise? The first response, no doubt, is stimulated ambition. This not only means that a person will perform a heavy task but also that happiness for the entire fatherland will be expected. Even if the fruit of this effort is not a source of happiness, this saying should express the fact of sacrifice—"Look and rejoice; see what heroes you have amongst you."

Soon thereafter comes a critical reflection, "Fine, fine, but let's not exaggerate," or "Agreed, but let's put the burden uniformly on everybody," or simply "Crap!" The critical reflection is accompanied by a sense of weariness. When little things assume too great an importance, it is an indication that reason is escaping from the world just like the air from a balloon. Something, somewhere, has lost its ordinary sense. What? Where? That is not known exactly. Not knowing is so much worse because now everything looks suspicious. The promises, instead of stimulating to action, tire and provoke laziness.

Persuasion is an integral component of governing. A style of governing expresses itself, to a large extent, through its style of persuasion. From the style of persuasion, one may form an opinion about what persuaders know about the people to whom they speak. One can more or less guess what vision of humanity persuaders carry in their minds. No one tries to persuade a vacuum. Everyone has a concept of "an abstract person" into which one puts the sum of one's knowledge of human fears and human desires for happiness. Sometimes, listeners find themselves in this abstract concept and know that the speech of persuasion is about them and to them. However, it often happens that the listener knows just this: "A frog is speaking to a frog."

It would be extremely interesting to find out what the "abstract person" of our television and other media of mass persuasion looks like—to find out between what promise of happiness and what fear these media place a person. What is this person most afraid of? What does this person want most? Once we have some idea of the answers to these questions, we could ask further whether and to what extent this person rises above the level of conditioned reflexes—reflexes that determine the behavior of a certain group that considers itself "pleasant friends" of real people?

I believe that the difference between the "abstract person" who is the publicist's average person and the concrete person of true reality is striking. "Who do they take us for?"—this is the characteristic reaction to the typical style of persuasion. On the one side, there is a vision of a creature that lives by reflexes. On the other side? What is on the other side? One must simply say— *free human beings,* simply and humanly free. These people live and walk on a different plane. Neither fears nor promises are the most important parts of their spiritual life. These do not even reach their knees. It turns out that true freedom is not a freedom among reflexes but the rising above reflexes.

How does one carry out a dialogue with these people?

I wonder whether I have to answer this question. Truly, the helplessness of my brothers-opponents is my opportunity. Thus, I say, "Excellent, gentlemen, excellent, carry on this way."

FAMILY

"WHAT SHALL we parents leave behind for our children?" In reply, we sometimes say, "If only they would not suffer as we do." The bitter recollection of our past rings in this saying. Some have in mind the times of war, others, the difficult days of the post-war reconstruction of the country; still others think of the hopeless times spent later in the lines in front of food stores. The basic intent here is clear; we have to make life *easier* for our young people. To make life easier means to ensure ham on the sandwich, to facilitate entrance to the university, to provide them their own place to live. But is this all? Some think secretly, "In the daily struggle to stay afloat, we lost, we slipped down; nothing is going to excuse our actions. Let us do at least whatever is needed for our children to have an easier life; someone must step into the mud so that others may stay clean." In this way there emerges a peculiar "family morality" born in times of darkness.

We do have, however, evidence of another ethos. The question is the same as above. The answer resounds, "Above all, let us not bring shame on our children; let them not be ashamed of their mothers and fathers." A child who is growing up and wants to learn directly from the mouths of witnesses the most recent history of Poland may pose the question, "What did you do in the summer of 1980?" or "On whose side was Daddy when the Polish October, June, March, arrived?" Children who see luxury surrounding them may become curious; "How did you, dear parents, acquire all this in a time of national poverty?" To be a father and a mother not only means to give life but also to be a bearer of the dignity of the family, of the family honor.

In recent months, a huge number of Polish families have faced a situation in which they had to decide what heritage should be passed on to their children. Should it be wealth plus a more-or-less clear sense of shame, or should it be pride in duty well fulfilled but without the signs of luxury? These decisions have not come easy. They have had to be made by young people, often without their own place to live, with small children to provide for—people just trying to get by in life. Strikes and meetings absorbed their minds, their hearts, and the remnants of their free time. Anxiety emerged: Is there any point in trying to repair the country but at the same time neglecting one's own family?

The fact that a large number of people gave a positive answer to this question testifies to the great maturity of young families. The issue was not only to provide milk and bread for their children but also to ensure that today's generation will be able to look directly and with a clear conscience into the eyes of tomorrow's generation and say, "Do your duty as we did ours." This problem cannot be solved once and for all. Each day presents us with the necessity for looking for a golden mean between time for our fatherland and time for our own family.

In days of crisis, the sense of national responsibility grows quicker then ever. The idea of Nation comes down from out of the clouds to earth. The simple truth reveals itself; the fate of one's own family is tied to the fate of the next family, and the fate of the family is the destiny of the nation. A sense of responsibility for the nation is not the negation of family consciousness but its expression. We are a great national brotherhood and the child of each family is the child of us all.

But this kind of consciousness of national responsibility is characterized by a certain one-sidedness. It has, above all, a defensive nature. We know that we should defend the values that are endangered. We also know, roughly, which values are involved. "Thou shalt not kill" changes into "Give milk to a child." "Thou shalt not give false witness" becomes "Write the truth in the newspaper" or "Speak the truth in school." The more basic the values that are threatened, the more widespread and sharp is the protest against the threat, and the stronger is the consciousness of the protesting human communion. This consciousness, however, becomes blurred and frayed when individual values or personal interests come into play.

In our times, the defensive consciousness is most frequently focused on the three key values: the right to just wages for work, the right to freedom, and the right to possess religious hope. The question of justice has been connected to the defense against exploitation of work. The problem of freedom has revealed itself as the defense of the right of assembly and of free expression of individual opinions. Defense of religious hope has found its expression in a concern about religious instruction, the freedom of the practice of religion, and life that is compatible with a Christian conscience. In the name of these three key values, albeit brought to reality in various ways, fathers and mothers temporarily abandoned some urgent family duties in the belief that by doing so they would not only improve the Commonwealth but would also be able to look with a clean conscience into the eyes of their children. They went away to rescue and then to return. They went away with a crowd, together with others, because the rights of all were being threatened.

In the difficult days of foundation building, the vision of things in which no one is able to replace either a father or a mother becomes sharper. There are words and gestures that belong to parents alone. If a child does not learn the meaning of these by looking at the faces of his father or mother, he will not learn them at any other time or in any other place. This is the cornerstone of the concrete duties of parents and can be summarized in a word—*testimony.*

They who fight for justice outside ought to practice justice within their own families: To everyone his due. They who fight for freedom cannot be tyrants in their own homes. They who stand in defense of the right to the truth cannot lie to those close to them. While reforming the world around us, we cannot overlook ourselves.

In this way we give testimony. At issue is not only action; at issue is testimony to the values in the name of which we act. Those who fight thieves but steal themselves do not give testimony, even though their fight may, within certain limits, be useful. Within the family, testifying is more important than acting. Children grow according to the testimony given them.

The sense of a double obligation—to the action and to the family—is not a light one. The greatest difficulty comes from the fact that not only I but others must be sacrificed. Can I force others to partake in my sacrifice? If the father dies, who will feed his child?

Each involvement must be accompanied by understanding. One should strive toward a clarification of the issues. All should know the values involved and know the purpose of the sacrifice. That is why one must speak out, explain. One must know how to listen to others' explanations. "What would you do in my place?" In this way, one broadens the imagination of society; one teaches people from childhood to think in communal categories. It may by painful, but it would be even more painful to live with the horizons of a mole. It has been said, "Carry one another's burdens and in this way fulfill God's law" (Gal. 6:2).

One should try, however, to avoid needless sacrifices. There is a certain paradox in this: It is easier to bear patiently with the absence of a father during a strike than with his absence due to a protracted meeting. In the case of a strike, most often, the issue is a great one. In the case of a meeting, it is often just listening to those who desire to "speak their mind." Today we learn democracy. Shall we also learn to hold shorter meetings?

From testimony and understanding come the ethos of the family. It consists of sensitivity to values and readiness for mutual help proper to each family. This ethos may occasionally be a heritage from one's antecedents—from father and mother, from grandparents and great-grandparents. This ethos forms the peculiar Polish aristocracy of spirit—an aristocracy in which all classes of the Commonwealth participate. In the last months, this heritage has been multiplied by a host of families of workers and peasants who are building a new Poland as a great Fatherland of Families.

ADVERSARY

A TRUCE with one's conscience is particularly demanding when one encounters an adversary. In such a case, who does not think of using force? Who does not wish to use fear as a tool of persuasion? However, this is not the point. To act according to the principle of revenge increases the number of graves but does not contribute to the growth of truth. I would compare the working of conscience to the action of planting trees. Someone plants a tree—one, a second, a third, many trees. From these trees grows a forest. The forest is. The forest exists, lasts. The reality of the forest cannot be disregarded. Whoever passes by will have to take into account the existence of the trees. A traveler will rest in the shade of the forest, a painter will paint a picture, a hunter will look for game. Conscience also plants a forest. Solidarity represents a huge forest planted by awakened consciences. Everyone must accept this reality. It is like the earth under our feet.

We know that forests have their enemies. How does the forest fight its enemies? The forest fights its enemies by growing and becoming an even larger forest. Solidarity of conscience fights its opponents by becoming more of a conscience and more of a solidarity. Everything else is but secondary.

This is significant; the Solidarity Movement fights for its rights by means other than that of "demonstration." People who participate in a demonstration take up banners and placards, write various words on the walls, shout slogans, and by so doing indicate what they are thinking. A demonstration is primarily shouting. The louder the shouts, the better the demonstration. The cry of the solidarity of consciences is not at all loud. This cry is accurate. This cry is often drowned out by other noises. In spite of this, it draws the attention of the nation. This cry achieves its effect not through volume but through accuracy. Forests also grow without noise.

It is significant that this conscience acts without appealing to fear. Today people abhor fear so much that they have not only ceased being afraid but also ceased frightening others. It seems as if frightening has been replaced by shaming. One takes a mirror and puts it in front of adversarys' faces so they can see for themselves what they are. "You were saying that you want to govern, but in fact, you plundered the forest." This is the hour of disgrace. After this, some lose all desire to govern, or even if they do not lose it, others are no longer able to take them seriously enough to be able to listen to them. Kings leave because they are not needed. The forest still grows.

Now, the question of a strike comes into full view. Here strike has a unique meaning, different from the one it has outside of our country's borders. What is this meaning?

A strike is a protest against the moral exploitation of work (see "Exploitation"). The consciousness of the moral exploitation of work reaches its peak at the moment when working people discover that they work *senselessly*. Senseless work may have several variants; the most common is wasted work. We work in vain. Either our work is fruitless—or the fruits of the work are too small to sustain and develop life—or there is no real need for the work being performed. We make a great effort, and nothing comes of it. We get up early, we go to bed late, we are exhausted; but our poverty constantly increases. From here, a pain and the beginning of a protest are born. When the work becomes senseless, a strike appears to be the only sensible action.

The stirring of protest does not yet mean that the protest will erupt. Protest erupts when something particular, something that moves the people, takes place. For example, the authorities decide to increase food prices drastically. Then the voices of the hungry—mothers, wives, children—will sound loudly. Working people behind their workbenches cannot remain deaf to this cry. Everyone knows "Something must be done now."

At this moment, a common conscience is born. People who want to do something good become members of a spontaneously formed communion of people of goodwill. They have love in their hearts for those for whom they work. They feel the taste of courage on their lips. They know, without special education, that right now something sensible is happening. In growing to the point of striking, they grow to their full humanity. Participation in *such* a strike becomes a moral act, that is, an act dictated by the order of the ethics of work. Humanity rises from the Fall and regains a human horizon and human dignity.

At the same time, during the strike, and somehow because of the strike, a new and particular attitude of the working person to the workplace crystallizes. From then on, the people become the true masters of their workplaces. They are at home there. They feel at home. They will not break windows, destroy machinery; they will not quit the "home." They demand that the workplaces they manage be used in a proper way. They repeat, "We are putting our home in order."

The issue is not what has been written on a piece of paper. The title of ownership is sealed, not by a signature, but by the work itself. The workplaces belong to those who have soaked them with their sweat and blood, those who have covered them with their concerns. Times of strike then are times that reveal the mystery of work. Work endows possession. A person wants to *give,* and because of that a person starts to *have.* The work of conscience is like the growing of a forest. The forest not only takes nutrients from the soil but also transforms the soil so it supports the growth. Leaves and needles fall from the trees and form the forest floor. In this way, the forest changes the character of the soil—the soil becomes the soil of the forest. In a similar way the workplace, thanks to work, becomes the place of working people.

A strike becomes a sensible act when work has become senseless. This is understandable; when work becomes senseless, it is only sensible to refrain from work. The issue is to return *sense* to work. At the same time, a strike reveals a few essential truths about human beings, especially about the working person. Let us recollect these truths.

We now know that it is not work that creates a working person but the working person who creates work, by giving it a proper sense. It is the working person who decides how to work—sensibly or senselessly. The working person confronts the authority, upon which the general system of work depends, with the key decision: Either it will govern work sensibly or itself become senseless authority, illusory authority, paper authority. Authority, if it wishes to be true authority, must serve the logic of work.

A strike also shows to whom the workplaces really belong. This refers to belonging according to the truth and not according to what is on paper. The essential power of a strike is not that it opposes someone but that it turns out to be a sensible action in a world that has lost sense.

In the new home grow new people. The new people build new homes. In the new home reigns the love of those *for* whom the working person works; here reign courage and social wisdom. There *is* a new feeling of dignity. In this way a forest grows. Everyone who enters it must realize that the forest *is.* A forest of this kind is the greatest treasure of the nation.

BETRAYAL

BETRAYAL is a cardinal sin against the solidarity of consciences. It is not so much betrayal understood as an abandonment of ideals as it is an outright betrayal of a human being. Betrayal is breaking the bonds of fidelity. Therefore we must ask ourselves, What is fidelity?

We shall not understand the essence of fidelity if we do not take into consideration that fidelity is an integral component of hope. Hope directs us toward the future—through hope the future becomes our spiritual value. Because hope directs us to future values, it allows us to overcome today's difficulties. Hope is born during times of trial, and it is a force that allows us to make it through these times. Hope has still another dimension, its human reference. There is always someone in whom I place my hope. When I arrange a meeting with a friend I trust him; I know that he will come. The source of my hope, its power and its light, is the person entrusted with my hope. I say, "In you I put my hope." From this moment the fidelity of the trustee will be the strength of my hope.

To betray means to break the bonds of trust.

A person's work is also an expression of a certain hope. Within work, too, we encounter an element of the entrusting of hope. Work is a dialogue. When I work I always work with some colleague in whom I have confidence. A sailor tosses a line from the deck of a boat and is confident that the dockworker will catch it. I trust that those for whom I work will not waste and will properly use the fruit of my work, that the knife whose point I sharpened for a familiar use will not be thrust into the heart of another human being. Finally, I trust those who have planned and who govern my work. I believe that they will not ask me to work senselessly. I make an effort to catch a lot of fish, and I trust that some of them will not be discarded because there are too many.

Into this threefold dimension of trust, betrayal can creep. What are the faces of treachery?

The betrayal of Judas is a symbol of the most tragic betrayal. It is betrayal by a co-worker, and it reaches the point of sending someone to his death. The issue here is not just that someone does not catch a line tossed to shore but that that person strikes directly at the one who tossed the line. Someone who belongs to the same community that I belong to is "betrayed to death." This betrayal can be enacted only by a co-worker. A prerequisite for this betrayal is "being with someone," "being-together-with someone." Our thoughts were akin, our motions were synchronized, we stood side by side bowing our heads before the same symbols. It is precisely because of the previous communion that the subsequent betrayal is possible. Had Judas not been admitted to participate in the life of the Teacher from Nazareth, there could not have been a betrayal. Condemnation to death came as an abuse of trust.

The treachery of a co-worker can have two forms—open, and hidden. Denunciation is an open form of betrayal. This is what Judas did. Denunciation means giving away someone's secret to another who—knowing this secret—will try to subjugate that person. Denunciation does not serve the truth; it serves enslavement. Denunciation is usually rewarded. Denunciation, by serving enslavement, is unethical. In rewarding it, one rewards immorality. Judas realized this and threw the pieces of silver at the feet of those who commissioned him.

Refusal to work together is a hidden form of betrayal. This, to some extent, would fit the case of Peter, who said, "I do not know this man." Peter did not pick up the line tossed to him. A worker works on the construction of an engine. From others, he receives ready-made parts. However, one of his co-workers makes parts imprecisely; as a result, the whole engine is no good. The one who made the part imprecisely in some way "denied" the others, betrayed them, failed the hopes entrusted to him. In this way, the work of many people has been wasted.

Work also requires trust between those of us who work and those for whom we work. When I buy bread I trust that the bread is not laced with poison. When I sell a knife to someone, I trust that person will not use this knife against me or someone else. The possibility of treachery that emerges here can also assume two forms.

It may be the treachery of one who sells bread. The bread may turn out to be bread with falsified ingredients. I buy bread with real money, but I receive false bread. This may happen with a radio, shoes, a car. The betrayal takes the form of cheating.

It may also be the treachery of the buyer. Someone buys a knife and kills his brother with it. Someone buys alcohol to get his guests drunk. The one who made the knife acted in good faith and with good intent. Here, treachery assumes the form of an "abuse" of good intentions, abuse of someone's work. Of good work and its good fruit, one makes evil use.

Finally, there is a third dimension to the entrusting of hope, the bond between those who project a comprehensive plan of work in a given society and those who carry it out. Here also exist trust and confidence. Betrayal on this plane expresses itself as a crisis of work. The people perceive work in this circumstance as senseless work. What good does it do when a fisherman exceeds the quota if there is no place to store the excess fish? What good does it do when people build a steel mill if the steel produced in it is more expensive and of poorer quality than the steel available on the open market? The good work of individuals at one level—the work of fishermen or the work of steelworkers—is a priori doomed on higher levels to be wasted. None of the particular efforts makes sense if the totality of the work has lost its sense.

This third kind of betrayal consists in condemning work to senselessness.

Solidarity of consciences is an ethical movement the basis of which is *fidelity*. Let us be faithful to each other. Let us be faithful to each other in spite of denunciations, in spite of denials of one another, in spite of the waste of one person's work by another, in spite of the abuse of work. Let us abandon senseless work. The call for fidelity is a form of struggle against the exploitation of one by another at the level of work. At issue is not only that the working person receive just compensation for work but also that the work itself be honest, that the worker works sensibly. Work is like conversation. For a conversation to be a conversation, one must speak the truth. So it is with work; for work to be work it must achieve its truth. Bread must be bread; a word, a word; a question and its answer must meet on the same plane.

Fidelity arises and grows where clear light reigns. In the darkness, everything becomes suspicious. We must see with whom we deal and what the problems are. We must be ready to reveal ourselves in total truth. The more we yearn for fidelity, the more forcefully we must repeat: "More light."

————

FATHERLAND

Every day we face the question of the fatherland. The fatherland comes to us like a gift. Simultaneously, the existence of the fatherland depends on us. Despite the fact that the fatherland is a gift to us, its fate depends on us. Indeed, the question of the fatherland looms over our conscience. We feel this; there is a Polish conscience within us. This conscience rules each one of us individually, and at the same time, it rules our entire nation. The voice awakens hopes that match the ordeal and courage that measures up to the courage of our fathers. The voice of Polish conscience leads us through the windings of history and points unmistakably to those values for which one must fight, as well as those that can be disregarded.

Conscience delineates within us the sphere of free choices available to us. Freedom within us is like an arena in which we can move safely. Thanks to conscience, license is transformed into freedom and freedom is no longer an ordinary understanding of and adaptation to necessity. Human beings are free because of the freedom that has been established in them by their consciences. The shape of freedom is not given to a person once and for all. It changes according to the dictates of conscience. The limits of Polish freedom are outlined by the Polish conscience. Everything that is below these limits is enslavement and degradation. Everything that is above these limits is utopia. Realistic Polish freedom is determined by the wise voice of conscience that knows the conditions of the people.

Polish conscience, by establishing freedom, chooses Poland. "Let Poland be Poland." [27] What does this mean? To choose Poland means to give testimony. Which Poland is our choice today? What is our testimony today? On what level do those values exist that Polish conscience wants to protect today?

The basic testimony revolves around the sense of human dignity. The concept of human dignity defies simple definition. Human dignity is a value that can be seen and felt but one about which it is difficult to speak. One can, however, turn attention toward this value by pointing out its context. The context of the concept of human dignity is human rights. Human dignity expresses itself through the rights afforded to human beings. What are those rights? Let us list some examples.

A human being has the right to possess the highest Hope—Hope that binds human beings and the human communion with God. It is irrelevant whether or not God exists, whether the stories of salvation after death are dreams or truth—these are issues of a different order. One can discuss them, dispute them, take different positions. The essential issue is the right to such a Hope. The point is that no one can deny anyone the right to have this Hope. One can argue about theory and the validity of arguments, but one cannot deny the right to the Hope. Such a denial is made by every act of discrimination against those who live according to this Hope. By a denial of this right, one takes aim at human dignity. We step below the limits marked out for us by the Polish conscience.

Human beings also have the right to sensible work. Senseless work, regardless of its form, strikes at the sense of dignity of the working person. It is a form of betrayal. Betrayal is forbidden! It is forbidden either through words or deeds—or refusal to act. The one who betrays slips below the level of conscience.

Human beings have the right to assemble, especially in an assembly that expresses the commonality of working people. Labor associations are not like a rose pinned to tattered garments. Work itself ties people to each other. Work is a conversation of many with many. The union of working people only expresses outwardly what is going on inside their work.

One could extend this list. Everything, however, concentrates on this single issue—human dignity. What is human dignity for us today? It is a form of human independence. The independent dignity of working people today represents the independence of Poland. Some would perhaps like to know how independent Poland is today. It is easy to see this. Poland is as independent as the Polish conscience is independent, as independent as are the Polish working people when once awakened by the voice of conscience.

When we choose the fatherland, we also choose our own history. The choosing of our own history means that we push certain events into the background and stand others before our eyes as an example. This is of great significance. When referring to history, one participates in the dignity of those whose deeds one continues. Whose deeds does the Polish conscience want to continue today?

Generally speaking, the Polish conscience wants to continue the work of those who created a spiritual national independence. Without belittling the courage of the Chrobrys[28] or the Sobieskis,[29] the examples of their military endeavors are overshadowed. To the forefront come the advocates of spiritual realities. We remember the works of Paweł Włodkowic,[30] who at the Council of Constance (1415)[31] defended the principles of international law against the advances of Teutonic Knights.[32] We recall the courage of the thought of Mikołaj Kopernik;[33] the courage of the theory of the social order of Frycz Modrzewski;[34] the works of the Commission of National Education;[35] the works of the Romantic poets, the theoreticians of science about life in society, the creators of popular movements. Conscience needs thought and for this reason feels a closeness with those who in this country "dared to think."

"Let Poland be Poland." Everything that is an illusion, a lie, an introduction of error, is below the level of conscience. The independence of Poland is a part of the independence of the truth. For this reason all who were born among us and came into our world to give a testimony of truth here are particularly close to us.

On the gate of the Gdańsk shipyard hung a portrait of John

Paul II.[36] Today this picture is an integral part of the image of our country. The portrait was a sign that "He is with us." What is the significance of this sign for the future?

Whatever we might say about the popes, one thing is certain; the popes know what history is. They know what truly lasts in history and what passes away like the grass in the autumn. The popes have a duty to remind us of what is indestructible, so that people and nations might tie their fates with what lasts. A pope's vantage point over the world is a special one. No one in the world looks at history and at the world from a point of view like that of the pope. No one has yet looked at Poland from this point of view and in *such a way* as did John Paul II. All knew, "He is with us."

The vision of John Paul II became a part of the Polish conscience. It is not always easy for a Pole to live with this vision. We know how Poles are. But it is also known that from this vision was born, and then was fixed, our present sense of dignity, our spiritual independence.

Choosing the fatherland today, we also choose this point of view on Poland. It does not mean that from now on everyone in Poland should be Catholic—No! This is not the issue. Faith is a grace, whereas freedom is a basic human right. The issue is that in this pope there is something that everyone can accept. What is it? It is this point of view on Poland, a vantage point from which one sees our country on the large canvas of a one-of-a-kind historical landscape. Having in front of us such a landscape of world history, we see more readily what in history lasts and what passes. Thus it comes easier to us to stand close to what lasts.

By this accent on the theme of today's independence of Poland, I close this cycle of reflections on the ethics of solidarity. I am aware of all the weaknesses of the text. The text was born in heated moments and was a spontaneous reply to what was happening. I wanted, as far as possible, to fulfill the duty of a Christian philosopher and to accompany the events with the light from the words of wisdom of philosophers. I had no desire to summon to anything, to establish anything, to induce anything. I wished only to describe the reality of a spirit being born. Life is wiser than people. So is the life of history. History lives in such a way that it awakens human consciences and in this manner defines an ethos that fits the emerging needs. Ethos is first. Ethos acts on people so that they might speak and act according to the ethos. Our duty is to listen. I have dared to go a step further and describe this ethos. Certainly, I would not claim to describe exactly what has happened and is happening.

OF THE SPIRIT OF
THE CONSTITUTION

(A sermon delivered during the outdoor mass on Wawel Hill on May 3, 1981)

It is our history that has charted the sense of our meeting today on Wawel Hill. We meet here on the anniversary of the promulgation of the Constitution of May Third[37] to pray together and through this prayer to strengthen our hope. There are many different prayers. There is a prayer of complaint, a prayer of joy; there is the asking for forgiveness, for bread, for deliverance from war and pestilence. What is our prayer like today on the Wawel? With what concerns have we come onto this Royal Hill?

It seems to me that our prayer today should be called a prayer of *feeling of responsibility.* We have come here carrying in our hearts a new feeling of responsibility. We always felt responsible—that is true—but somehow differently, not so deeply, not so broadly. We often stood to one side, like those who are lame and powerless, as we watched passively the parade of history. Today, it is different. We feel that we are standing in the midst of a powerful current. We are no longer the "popular masses"; we are a part of a nation. Everything that concerns the nation passes through our nerves, hearts, and minds. We have been maturing in the midst of strikes. We have been maturing in the midst of prayer. We feel today that we are truly responsible for a real nation and a real tomorrow. This new burden of responsibility is not an easy one, but it has meaning. With this new feeling of responsibility we are coming today onto Wawel Hill to disclose ourselves to God and the Queen of Poland.[38]

What does it mean to be responsible? To be responsible means to be *faithful*. The source of the feeling of responsibility is fidelity. Today the core of our cause is fidelity. We know one thing: "Everything is permitted except betrayal." Everywhere today we learn about fidelity. When we read the gospel, we read it as a great textbook of fidelity. In the same way we read our own history. When we wish to exclaim the greatness and the glory of humanity, we say, "We are beings who are capable of fidelity." When we want to give an example of the greatest guilt of humanity, we point to Judas. When we want to name the greatest guilt of a Pole, we say, "Targowica."[39] Today, Wawel Hill becomes for us the Hill of Fidelity. We have now but one desire, to return to our homes with a wiser feeling of responsibility, with a deeper fidelity.

Let us take an imaginary journey into the distant, yet still living, past. The Constitution of May Third was born in the period of our downfall, defeat, and national disaster. These were bad times, these were dark times. Not only Poland, but also other countries, were living at a crossroad for them. In France, the blood of king and of subject as well was spilled. In other countries it was the blood of subjects. Poland was searching for her *middle* road out of this crisis. In times like these, one has to find within oneself only one thing—the great courage to think. The constitution was created by people of whom it would be said later, Those were people who "dared to think." For this reason to us the constitution is primarily a symbol of thinking—Polish heroic thinking. The strength of this constitution lies in the strength of the thought that created it. *"Sapere auso"*—"They dared to think."

At the very beginning there was thinking. Not far from here are the walls of Jagiellonian University.[40] Within these walls since time immemorial the sphere of Polish thinking has been shaped. We know well the names of its pillars. Here is the figure of Paweł Włodkowic, who at the Council of Constance would have to defend the moral rights of Poland to the lands taken by the Order of Teutonic Knights. It was not enough to win the Battle of Grunwald; it was further necessary to show the ethical sense of that battle, to prove that the fight was for a just cause. The deed of the knight had to merge with the deed of the thinker. In the walls of the university we see the figure of Mikołaj Kopernik who "stopped the sun and moved the earth." "The Polish people produced him." The heroism of this thought is commonly recognized today. Is it an accident that such an idea was born in a country of tolerance and pluralism, where no one had to be afraid of being himself? The Polish sphere of thinking also includes others—Frycz Modrzewski, Jan Kochanowski,[41] and Piotr Skarga.[42] From this current emerged the thinkers of the century of the constitution; from here came the writers of the constitution. They dared to think! Polish thinking blended criticism with building; it awakened doubts, but only to rebuild certainty. This thinking was able to inflict pain, even great pain, but did so not to sow despair but to heal. At the core of this thinking was a sacred word—Truth.

Today, we stand here with our renewed feeling of responsibility. We ask each other what it means to be faithful. Our answer comes from the spirit of the constitution. It means to *have the courage to think*. It means to put in the very center of our thoughts the sacred word—Truth. Today, we see this clearly and we feel it well; a lie would be our Targowica—a lie in print, in the press, in school, in the walls of the Jagiellonian University.

One must restore to thinking its proper dimensions. At the

beginning is thinking. Workers today become the masters of factories; farmers become the masters of the land. It is necessary that physicists become the masters of physics; economists, the masters of economics; and it is necessary to leave philosophy to philosophers. No one can farm on someone else's land. The sphere of Poland is not only the tract in which we walk but also the space in which we breathe, because "a Pole does not live by bread alone."

The Constitution of May Third opens to us another historical perspective. It exposes, for the first time on such a scale, the meaning of human work and the value of working people in the life of the nation. We know that not everything in it has achieved its final formulation. However, the constitution gave us a beginning, and beginnings—as we well know—are the most difficult. The question of the working people that was put forth by the constitution would return. It would return in the Manifesto of Połaniec[43] issued by Tadeusz Kościuszko,[44] it would return in the works of writers, poets, thinkers—it will always return in association with those beginnings. Our meeting here today is just such a return to the source. What is our concern on this occasion? The issue in those days was not only the granting of land to the peasants, the introduction of social justice, bread for both the humble and the great. The issue was, primarily, that any work carried out in this land of ours be *work with sense.*

A working person must work with sense. People work sensibly when their work binds them with others rather than separating them from others. Work has to be a *form* of *fidelity* of one person to another.

The events of the past year are still fresh in our memory today. What was this mutiny in Poland all about? Against what was it directed? Today, it is clearly visible that the mutiny was directed against the betrayal that took up residence in the very midst of our world. Someone here betrayed someone, and from this betrayal the senselessness of our work was born. Senseless work is an extreme form of the exploitation of one person by another. It is simply the degradation of the human dignity of the worker.

When human work becomes senseless, the only reasonable behavior is to strike. The strike becomes a testimony to fidelity. One strikes in such a situation to return sense to human work so that the work again becomes a form of human fidelity. This is how the ethos of Polish work looks today, an ethos formed by the conscience of solidarity.

This ethos also comes from the spirit of the constitution. Our beginnings were there. To break the bonds with those beginnings means to betray. Today, every senseless gesture of a worker, every fruitless act of a farmer, every fruit of honest work thrown into the mud, would be what Targowica was for the constitution.

Today we say, "constitution." "Constitution" means that definite boundaries between betrayal and fidelity have been drawn. Now it is known where something begins. There is an extraordinary power in this constitution. From now on whoever in this country shall be against the constitution shall not be of the spirit of this country. Whoever wants to be faithful to this country will have to take to heart the boundaries between betrayal and fidelity as charted by this constitution.

Wawel Hill on which we pray today becomes our Fidelity Hill. We meet here today in common prayer of responsibility for the sacred value of Truth and for work full of sense. Responsibility can be only where fidelity is. We are faithful to ourselves. We do not want to lie to ourselves. We do not want to be lied to. In our land, we want to do work that joins. Such are we today on this Wawel Hill of Fidelity. As such we disclose ourselves before God and the Queen of Poland.

Something else can be added to this, and it is necessary to say it because it is the truth. Some carry it within themselves as a credo, others carry it as their hope, others as their deepest prayer. It must be said briefly because the issue is brief; this time there shall not be Targowica. Today, fidelity to the spirit of the constitution has become the conscience of the entire nation.

In this spirit let us now proclaim our *Credo* . . .

POLISH WORK IS SICK

*(A homily delivered in Olivia Hall during the mass
preceding the second day of the Solidarity Congress and, by
the resolution of the First National Congress of Delegates
of NSZZ Solidarność, included in the official records of the
congress)*

Nothing like this has ever before happened in this
land. What is the extraordinary nature of today's meeting? It is
not easy to answer this question. We all feel it; this is a historic
place, this is a historic anniversary; something is being built:
Here is Poland. But what is it that is so extraordinary? It seems
that I will touch the heart of the matter if I say that for the first
time in our history we have undertaken, on such a scale, a work
upon work. Yes indeed, this is our goal, work about work; this
has never happened before on such a scale. Until now, most
frequently the attention of Poles was drawn to the question of
what to do. What should we do so that Poland might be independent? What to do so there will be more bread? What to do so
there will be more books? Today it is different. One cannot say
that the question of what to do has ceased to be timely. It is still
an important issue, but how to do it has moved into first place.
The quality of work has become the issue. Our meeting today
should be considered as an event in the history of the culture of
Polish work.

It should be kept in mind that, above all, human work has its
own past, its own history. Our forefathers worked differently
than we do. In days gone by, land was plowed with a wooden
stick, and only later did the plow replace the wooden stick. Pre-
viously, a horse was the helper of the plowman, today a machine
serves this purpose. The history of work is the history of tools of

work. But this is not all; the history of work is also shaped by the mutual bonds between people who somehow are joined by the work they perform. Who works with whom is important. Once, a father worked, and with him his family. Today, the communion of working people has widened. A reciprocity has crossed the borders of villages and towns and the frontiers of the state. I do not know who made the pen that I have in my pocket. Whoever made the pen has a part in the work that I am doing; he or she is my co-worker—a link in an enormous chain.

So the tools change and the reciprocity widens. Work is like a river that grows bigger by collecting its tributaries. We are near the estuary of the Vistula.[45] The Vistula collects the waters of most of the rivers of Poland. Our congress today collects the separate streams of Polish work into one river and intends to examine them closely. It wants to understand this Polish work, to define it, to capture its essence, and then to undertake the activity—the first activity of this type in the history of Poland—of a work upon work.

To begin this activity properly, we must look at the issue from above, like looking from the peaks of the Tatras,[46] where the waters of the Vistula have their beginning. The very liturgy of the Mass encourages us to do this. In a moment, during the Offertory, we shall hear these words: "Blessed are you, Lord, God of all creation, through your bounty we have received bread—fruit of the earth and work of human hands—which we offer you." And the same with wine: "We have received wine—fruit of the earth and work of human hands." This bread and this wine shall become in a moment the body and blood of the Son of God. This has a deep meaning. Thus the ultimate horizon of work is unraveled for us. Were it not for human work, there would be no bread or wine. Without bread and wine, there would not be among us the Son of Man. God does not come to us through a creation of nature alone, holy trees, water, or fire. God comes to us through the first creation of culture—bread and wine. Work that creates bread and wine paves the way toward

God. But every work has a part in this work. Our work, too. In this way our work, the work of each one of us, paves the way to God.

The Vistula also brings water here from the Tatra Mountains. There, as we know, one is close to the heavens. The water of the Tatras is clean; in this clean water the heavens are reflected. Such is also a sense of our work. In this work, heaven is also reflected. The unique quality of Polish work has been and still is that in it heaven is reflected more often. God brought fortune to Polish work because this work is the Polish road to God. We must guard and protect this reflection as the apple of our eye, because this reflection gives the deepest meaning to human work. Without this reflection, one may lose the feeling of the meaning of one's work. One may also lose the feeling of being a Pole.

Work is also a reciprocity. It is not only reciprocity between people but reciprocity between people and God—God, who through his grace sanctifies the world.

From the mountaintops, we must look at our daily routines. Polish work is sick. The reason for our being here today is that Polish work is sick. The volume of work is great like the Vistula, but also like the Vistula, it is polluted. Today, we pose the question Why is Polish work sick? This is not easy to answer, but certain facts are clear. Work in Poland, instead of deepening reciprocity, instead of being a plane of humanity, became a plane of controversy, disagreement, and even betrayal. The waters of the Vistula are dirty. The waters of the Vistula are even blood-stained. We are here to cleanse the waters of the Vistula. We are laboring over work so that work might again become a plane of agreement, harmony, and peace.

Our concern is the independence of Polish work. The word *independence* must be understood properly. It does not aim at breaking away from others. Work is reciprocity, it is agreement, it is a multifaceted dependence. Work creates a communion. But within this communion and reciprocity, everyone must remain himself; a blacksmith, a blacksmith; a teacher, a teacher; a shipyard worker, a shipyard worker. To be independent means to be oneself. The very development of a work culture demands independence.

In spite of all, Polish work is independent. Work is independent when it bears fruit that cannot be faked. The fruit of independent Polish work were the masterpieces of the Romantic poets, Mickiewicz, Słowacki, Norwid,[47] Krasiński.[48] The fruit of independent Polish work is the writing that is also becoming the basis of European humanism—the encyclical of John Paul II *Redemptor hominis.*[49] The poetry of Czesław Miłosz is also such fruit. The social movement of "Solidarność" is such fruit too. One could multiply these examples.

We think also about the independence of Poland. Today, the problem has a different meaning than it had in the nineteenth century. The key to an independent Poland is a work about work, the pondering over a work culture. The key to the country's independence is today the independence of Polish work.

Sitting here among you in the Cathedral of Oliva and listening to the words of the Primate of Poland[50] about the fatherland, I remembered an old story. After the failure of the November Uprising,[51] a few ragged men found themselves on the streets of Paris—defeated, feuding, without hope of returning home. France gave them sanctuary out of pity. It seemed that they were doomed to a slow death. Those people began their work; they said of themselves proudly, "We are living history." And history proved them right. Everything passes, but work endures. It lasts because it is a fruit of reciprocity.

It seems to me that today I have the right to repeat these words. We know how difficult it is. We know how dark it is. We are familiar with all the ghosts of the night and the screams by day. But in those bygone days, it was even more difficult. The government was against them. All the powers of Europe were against them. Nonetheless, it was they who were right. Because historically it is not the one who has power that counts but the one who is right. Work flows like a river. A river, especially the Polish rivers, always finds its way to the sea.

For that reason, we are living history. A living history means one that bears fruit. Christ has said, "Let the dead bury their dead" (Matt. 8:22). Thus, let us do the same. Let us become occupied with bearing fruit. Let the water in the Polish Vistula become clean and independent—like the water in the Polish Five Lakes[52] in the Tatra Mountains.

THE TIME OF ROOTING

(A sermon delivered in Gdańsk on September 27th, 1981, during the First Congress of Solidarność)

TODAY, we are at the brink of the second phase of our work upon work. As before, we wish in a prayerful contemplation to entrust to God what he has put into our hands—our hope. We look today toward a future like those who have planted a forest. The future growth of the forest depends on how they planted the trees. We are full of hope but, at the same time, full of trepidation. This is normal. The issue facing us is to waste neither soil nor trees.

We feel the eyes of our compatriots turned on us. Some look at us with confidence, others with worry, still others with doubt or even fear. The key question for everyone emerges, Can we transform our Polish hopes into reality, especially the hope for wise and independent work? The trees of hope have many flowers, and on those trees flowers bloom easily. The crucial problem is, however, rooting. If the tree of hope does not find proper soil, it will wither regardless of how beautiful its flowers are. Now the time of rooting has come. Shall we rise to the task?

It is amazing! It is amazing how much our work about work became similar to what has been called "evangelizing" or "announcing the Good News." Evangelizing is also a work of rooting hopes. The hopes were numerous, like the flowers on a tree. However, not all of these were honest hopes. Christ tells us that the words of the Good News are like seeds that fall on the ground; one falls on sand, another on the path, another on stone (Mark 4:1-9). How much effort was needed to organize the hopes of the people who gathered around Jesus! Some wanted to be in Jesus' Kingdom close to his throne. Others wanted a new miracle of the multiplication of the loaves. Peter drew out a sword to fight. Above the whole landscape, a threatening shadow loomed—the picture of dead hope, the hope of Pharisees, hope drowned in its form. How does one root a hope to save it from becoming a fairy tale or from becoming petrified? This was a concern of Christ, and it still remains a worry of those who work on the Good News.

Today, during our prayer, our work about work comes into contact with the concern of Christ; we want to take something from the wisdom of this concern. What truth emerges from this encounter? The truth about human hope discloses itself before us. One can take bread from a man, and that man can sustain hunger for a long time provided only that his hope keeps him alive. Conversely, a man may have a lot of bread, but he will die if deprived of his hope. We do not know who has chosen what. At one time we may think that we have chosen our hope, but when we look closer, it appears that hope has chosen us. The gospel says, "You did not choose me but I have chosen you that you might go and bear fruit and your fruit will last" (John 15:16). We did not choose the Polish hope, it is a hope that has chosen us, and we have enjoyed this choice. In the past we began to serve this hope. Today, we come into touch with a great epoch of our history. At the turning points of history the basic truths are always the same. Common to these moments, above all, is the truth about the power of hope. Where, in what ground, in what kind of soil, should we root our hopes to make them stronger than death? We must ask ourselves these questions at a time in which we feel the burden of rooting our hopes.

John Paul II has written in his encyclical,[53] "Above all, work has the characteristic of binding people—this is the essence of its social power, the power of building a communion. Ultimately, those who work and those who govern the means of production or own them must somehow join with each other in this communion" (par. 74). It has been said here that work is a force. Work itself is a force. There is some kind of internal logic in work, some spirit of work. In the bosom of work lives its wisdom. Toward what does this wisdom embodied in work strive? It strives toward a communion of people. Work is, above all, an agreement. The more a work is work, the more such a work is independent, and the more it represents an agreement. A spirit of solidarity is the spirit of work. Human solidarity is not a supplement to work but a flower produced by the wisdom of work.

If our hopes are to last, they must be rooted in the wisdom that governs work, in the logic of work, in its spirit. Work itself will always call out to be truly a work. Work does not want to be a lie, an illusion, or treachery. Work by its very nature strives toward its own independence, that is, toward an agreement. Our hopes, our "hopes in solidarity" should be an *expression* of this call of work. It is not we who call but this; this is the logic of work, its wisdom that speaks through our voices.

The might of our hopes shall always be greater than the power of death, as long as we succeed in rooting our hopes in the power of the agreement of work. Then the forest will grow on its own, because the wisdom of the forest wants it so.

There is one more source of human hopes; the kind of soil on which these hopes grow. Noble trees require rich soil. What is the soil that our hope for independent work needs in order to grow? One must define this soil by a single word—*conscience.*

Every deed is a permanent deed only when it is based in the power of the human conscience. A deed supported by other forces is transient and destined a priori for destruction. Our problems today—the problem of the independence of work and the problem of an agreement through work—shall have a chance to be resolved when they become the concerns of the conscience of people—small and great, young and old, contemporary and future. Our basic problem is not an economic one; neither is it political. Economics and politics are only derivative problems. Our basic problem is a problem of conscience. At issue is for conscience to begin to govern our *entire* work. I repeat: our entire work and not only the work of some people.

Only hopes supported by our human conscience have the power to last. I believe that today we may lose everything, but if we succeed only in planting the idea of independent Polish work in the human conscience we shall have fulfilled our task. But if we do not achieve this, what shall we have gained from all our other victories?

Every work of rooting hopes is accompanied, as a warning, by the shadow of Palestinian Pharisaism.[54] Originally, Pharisaism was also a hope of Israel, but later the hope destroyed itself by stiffening its form. Instead of nurturing hearts, hope began to build a prison for the heart, and in this way the hope was changed into a mere formalization of the form. This has been repeated more than once. At the beginning of the nineteenth century, in the period of revolution and the Napoleonic wars,[55] G. W. Hegel, an outstanding philosopher of hope, at the time sharply criticized those who carelessly led human hopes to a wilderness of fairy tales and petrification. He wrote, "These kinds of ideal beings and aims fell apart like empty words that elevate hearts but leave the mind empty, words that are edifying but do not build anything." Hope in the wilderness. An artificial flower attached to a tree. Such a sight perhaps moves the heart, but it leaves the mind empty. Such a hope crumbles away like the hope of those who wanted to be found near the throne of Jesus, or those who demanded a second miracle of the multiplication of loaves—or like the hope of Peter, who reached for his sword. An excited heart but an empty mind.

Honest hope is different. Its power is the power to build a communion. Its voice is the voice of conscience.

We are here to pray together according to our conscience. During prayer we stand before the face of God. But not only this.

During prayer, a human being faces another human being. Let us not forget this. We remember the day when we gathered here for the first time. We remember the faces of the people surrounding the cathedral and on the streets. As long as we live, we shall remember those faces and the hope that was in their eyes. At prayer, we also face those people. We stand before the face of the whole of Poland.

Let us not forget; they will take a measure of their solidarity from our solidarity; the wisdom of this gathering shall be the measure of their wisdom; they will shape the voice of their conscience after the voice of your conscience.

Let us remember; during prayer a human being faces not only God but also another human being. This human being wants to see in the other the measure of himself. Do not forget. Whatever you say and do today—you are a measure.

AFTERWORD

"A LIE IS A DISEASE of speech," writes Father Józef Tischner, scholar and philosopher, chaplain of our union during the Solidarity Congress in Gdańsk. In September 1981, we talked a great deal about lies, about falsehood, about how to liberate ourselves from the demagoguery and propaganda schemes imposed on us for many years. Olivia Hall shall remain the symbol of this cleansing for a long time to come.

Father Tischner's book, for which I was asked to write an afterword (what an amazing task for a worker!), recounts the basic concepts utilized during innumerable meetings, conventions, demonstrations, and discussions, and which we still use today in personal conversations and underground publications. The book recalls the meaning of words that in my country were deprived of their proper content by propaganda and given a totally different sense, an Orwellian one.

When, in August 1980, a general strike was in progress in Gdańsk, party/government newspapers frantically sought deceptive and euphemistic terms to refer to this event. They wrote, "On the seacoast, spotty interruptions of work have taken place" or, "An irregularity of supplies has been noticed." Television reporters said, "There are certain breaks in production." Still, in spite of these troubles, it was maintained that under the party's leadership, the country was "marching toward a better future."

Obviously, the issue here was not only about words; the words simply manifested a fear of the truth—truth, suppressed for so long, that exploded with great force. The newspaper prattle was intended to hide the thousands of idle factories and the people in them, full of rebellion and hope. This propaganda had still one more, very characteristic aim: it was supposed to persuade people that those disruptions of work and irregularities were caused not by the workers, nor even by specific people, but by "the work force," anonymous and impersonal. The continuous references to production and its plunging levels demonstrated the role assigned to the workers: that of a tool that cannot strike, after all, since tools do not strike.

How it really was at that time we all know. Millions of people were shedding the invisible veneer of a lie and breaking the equally invisible barrier of fear. It was repeated loudly and thousands of times: Strike! Strike! Strike!—a taboo word, a word that they tried to suppress all too unsuccessfully.

Two years have passed; the martial law authorities have delegalized Solidarity. Today's grim reality does not resemble, at least at face value, those days. What, then, is left today of our aspirations, and what will happen in the future? The answer to this will be easier after reading Józef Tischner's book, and the effort to do so is worthwhile. He writes about things that still flow through the minds, and even more through the hearts, of my compatriots. Polish society submitted to sheer force, but it will not accept the argument that this force was its salvation.

Today, as before, the world of propagandistic illusion threatens us; it is supposed to exhaust us and deprive us of hope. This is one side of the reality here. But there is also another side: millions of people in Poland now know that nothing sensible can be built or reformed without dialogue and agreement. Juggling words and concepts that have no meaning is useless. Today's Solidarity is a communion of the people who do not wish to participate in a lie. This is the simplest ethic of the common working people.

Lech Walesa

EXPLANATORY NOTES

1. Wawel Hill is a low hill situated on the right bank of the Wisła (Vistula) River at the city of Kraków (Cracow). Initially a stronghold occupied the top of the hill, but after the eleventh century it gradually became the seat of Polish kings; finally, Bolesław (Boleslaus) III (1102–1138) transferred the capital of Poland to Kraków. Wawel remained the ceremonial royal residence even after Zygmunt (Sigismundus) III Vasa (Waza) in 1599 moved the capital from Kraków to Warszawa (Warsaw). The present complex consists of a magnificent Renaissance castle and the cathedral (see note 10). The castle is a branch of the national museum, and most of its rooms are furnished in the style of the Renaissance period. The cathedral is the metropolitan church of the archbishops of Kraków. The entire complex is surrounded by medieval walls and towers. Because the castle and the cathedral both contain numerous historical treasures and artifacts, they are considered to be a symbol of Polish statehood.

2. The Piasts were the first recorded Polish dynasty. The origins of this line reach back to the ninth century and are shrouded in legends that suggest that the founder of the dynasty was a simple crofter or homesteader (see note 19) who was elevated to his office by divine intervention. The first recorded ruler of the dynasty, Mieszko I, who was born in 920, was merely a prince who had to acknowledge the suzerainty of the German emperors over his domain. In 966, Mieszko introduced the practice of Christianity, and to protect the integrity of his state and assure its survival, he placed it under the Holy See. The first crowned king, Bolesław the Brave (992–1025), received his crown (1000) from Otto III, the German emperor, and his regency was recognized and confirmed by Pope Sylvester II. The last Piast, Kazimierz (Casimir) the Great (1333–1370), originally named his nephew, Louis the Great of Hungary, from the House of Anjou, as his successor. Later, the king changed his mind and made his grandson Kazimierz of Szczecin his heir; these plans were frustrated, however, by Louis. The lateral branches

of the Piast dynasty ruled Mazovia until 1526 and various Silesian principalities until 1675.

3. The Jagiellons were the second dynasty of Polish kings. The founder of the dynasty was Władysław (Wladislaus) Jagiełło (1386–1434), the grand duke of Lithuania (see note 8), who was baptized and crowned king in 1386 in fulfillment of the Treaty of Krewo (1385). According to this treaty, Jagiełło was required to convert to Christianity and introduce it to Lithuania before he could marry queen of Poland Jadwiga (Hedwig) of Anjou (1384–1399) and become co-ruler of Poland, with their children becoming heirs to the Polish throne. Through the person of the monarch, this arrangement created a union between Poland and Lithuania. The union was finalized in Horodło (1413), where it was established that the two countries would have a common ruler and common laws. The last king of the dynasty was Zygmunt (Sigismundus) II August (1548–1572), who refined the union by the Treaty of Lublin (1569). This treaty established that the two countries should have a common parliament and common institutions, but separate armies. The age of the Jagiellons was the golden age of Polish culture and economy. Members of the Jagiellonian house at one time or another ruled Hungary and Bohemia and were related to the Swedish dynasty of Vasa. Although the dynasty formally expired in 1572, it was continued in the person of the sister of Zygmunt II August, Queen Anna (1576–1586), who was also the wife of King Stefan (Stephen) Batory (1576–1586), the prince of Transylvania. Anna and Stefan were elected as rulers of Poland after the short reign of Henryk Walezy (Henry II of Valois), who had decamped to become Henry III of France. The blood of the Jagiellons was also in the veins of the next Polish dynasty, Vasa, since its founder in Poland was Zygmunt III (1587–1632), the son of John III of Sweden and Katarzyna (Catharine) Jagiellonka, the sister of Zygmunt II August. Zygmunt III was also king of Sweden (1592–1599).

4. Adam Mickiewicz (1798–1855), the most prominent Polish Romantic poet, studied at Wilno University and later became a school teacher. He was arrested and imprisoned in 1823 by the Russians for his attempts to preserve the Polish language and culture, which was discouraged by the Russians. He was found guilty and was sentenced to deportation to the interior of Russia. While in Russia, he met many progressive Russians, among them the great poet Aleksandr Pushkin. In 1829, he was permitted to leave Russia and traveled to Germany, Switzerland, Italy, and France. After an un-

successful attempt to reach Poland during the November Uprising (1830–31, see note 51), he joined Polish emigrés in Saxony and Paris (1832–34). It was during this period that his best works were written: in prose, *The Books of the Polish Nation and of the Polish Pilgrimage;* a drama of fantasy, *Forefathers' Eve* (this is an incorrect translation; it more properly would be *Beggars' Eve*); and the epic poem *Mister Thaddeus.* Even though he continued to write poetry, the remainder of his life was dominated by the succession of mental and physical turmoils suffered by an exile. He became editor of the French magazine *La Tribune des Peuples.* During this time, he became a religious mystic; later he tried to organize a Polish military legion (during the revolution of 1848, and again during the Crimean War, 1855). It was in this last effort that he met his death during a cholera epidemic in Istanbul. His remains were removed to Poland and laid to rest in the Kraków (see note 10) cathedral among the kings and heroes of the Polish nation. Mickiewicz was a great patriot as well as a man of progressive ideas in his contemporary Europe.

5. Juliusz Słowacki (1809–1849) was one of the foremost Polish Romantic poets, along with Adam Mickiewicz (see note 4) and Zygmunt Krasiński (see note 48). Born in Krzemieniec, he was educated at Wilno University and initially became an office clerk. By the time of the November Uprising (1830–31, see note 51), he was diplomatic emissary to England and remained in England as an emigré after the uprising was crushed. He traveled to Switzerland, Italy, Greece, Palestine, and Egypt and eventually settled in France. Highly educated and familiar with the works of the great poets and writers both past and contemporary, he is considered the most sophisticated Polish poet and the master of Polish poetry. He has often been called the Polish national bard. In his poetry, which deals with the perennial question of good and evil, one can find the influence of Shakespeare, Dante, and Byron. His works range from epics to lyric poems to dramas. Even though he was often considered to be self-centered and mystical, he was actively involved in the social and political events of the Europe of his day. In fact, he took great interest in the "People's Spring" revolutionary movement of 1848. He died of tuberculosis in Paris. His remains were finally removed to Poland in 1927, where they rest in Wawel cathedral (see note 10) among the remains of the kings and heroes of Poland.

6. Stanisław (Stanislaus) of Szczepanow (Szczepanowski) was the

bishop of Kraków at the time of Bolesław the Bold (1058–1079). The bishop and the king clashed on an issue that is not entirely clear today. According to some sources, the bishop chastised the king for abandoning his duties, and the king accused the bishop of high treason. The bishop excommunicated the king. In return, the king's tribunal sentenced the bishop to death. Legend maintains that the bishop was killed by the king's mercenaries at the foot of the altar while celebrating mass. An aura of sanctity surrounded the bishop, and in 1253 he was canonized and became the patron saint of Poland.

7. Bolesław the Bold (1058–1079), in an attempt to rebuild the kingdom of his great-grandfather, Bolesław the Brave, allied himself with Pope Gregory VII and the Hungarian kings Geza I (1074–1077) and László I (1077–1095), who were both adversaries of the German king and later emperor, Henry IV (1056–1105). To counteract German expansion and to strengthen the papacy, Bolesław the Bold conquered the Kievan Principality and placed Izaslaw, who supported union between Kiev and the Roman church, on its throne. It was during the Kievan war that Bolesław fell into conflict with Stanisław, the bishop of Cracow (see note 6). The execution of Stanisław led to strong opposition to Bolesław , who was forced to abdicate in 1079 and go into self-imposed exile. He died in 1081, either in Hungary or Carinthia.

8. Władysław Jagiełło, grandson of Giedymin (Gediminas) and son of Olgierd (Algirdas), became the grand duke of Lithuania by imprisoning his uncle Kiejstut (Kęstutis) and exiling his cousin Witold (Vytautas). In 1385, he made the Treaty of Krewo, in which he agreed to accept Christianity and marry Queen Jadwiga of Poland, thereby becoming the king of Poland (see note 3). The resulting Polish-Lithuanian union created a great European power that lasted for nearly two centuries. After the death of Queen Jadwiga, he married three more times and produced sons by his fourth wife. For these sons he secured the inheritance of the Polish throne, thus launching the Jagiellonian dynasty. The Treaty of Horodło (1413) established a close formal union between Poland and Lithuania and determined that the two countries would have a king and a grand duke, respectively. These regents were to be chosen by mutual consent of the nobility of the two countries.

9. The Battle of Grunwald was fought on June 15, 1410, near the villages of Grunwald and Tannenberg. In this battle, the Teutonic Order (see note 32) and its allies, led by Grand Master Ulrich von

Jungingen, faced the armies of Poland, Lithuania, and Ruthenia and a small detachment of Bohemian Hussites, all under the joint command of King Władysław Jagiełło (see note 8) and Grand Duke Witold. Although the battle ended in the total defeat of the Teutonic Order, it did not end the conflict of the opposing parties. Subsequent wars in 1414, 1422, and 1454 eventually led to the Second Treaty of Toruń (1466), which effectively ended the power of the Teutonic Order, through the partitioning of its holdings and subjugating it to the Polish monarchs.

10. Wawel cathedral is the church of the metropolitan archbishop of Kraków and is located within the confines of Wawel castle. This magnificent Renaissance edifice has been the place of coronation and burial of many Polish kings. Its treasury was the repository of the royal paraphernalia until they were stolen by the Prussians in 1795. Along the aisles of the cathedral are beautiful sculptured marble tombs of the early kings and queens of Poland. The tombs of the later kings and their families are in the crypt, as are the tombs of many great Poles. A huge bell, called Zygmunt, which was cast from captured enemy cannon, is suspended in the spire. The bell is sounded on important religious and national days.

11. Gdańsk is an ancient seaport city at the mouth of Wisła (Vistula) River. The city was originally built by the northern Slavs and was a part of Poland ruled by autonomous princes. The city was captured through treachery in 1308 by the knights of the Teutonic Order. Although the knights had been summoned to help regain control of the city, they instead slaughtered the Polish and local garrisons and took possession of the city, renaming it Danzig. The city was returned to Poland in 1466 but was later retaken by Prussia during the second partition in 1793 (see note 20). After World War I, Gdańsk was declared a Free City (Freie Stadt Danzig) in economic union with Poland. It was captured by the Germans during the early days of World War II and incorporated into the Reich. Heavily damaged during the war, Gdańsk became part of Poland after the defeat of the Nazis. In 1970, shipyard workers in Gdańsk demonstrated against Communist rule and were attacked by armed troops. An undisclosed number of workers were shot to death (see note 14). In 1980, the shipyard workers again went on strike and forced the Communist authorities to sign an agreement that led to the birth of the Solidarity Trade Union.

12. Szczecin is an ancient port city at the mouth of the River Odra. It was the See of the Pomeranian princes who were related to the Piast

dynasty. Although the Szczecin principality was subject to German emperors and Brandenburg electors, its ducal family and inhabitants were largely Slavic. Upon the extinction of its old ducal dynasty, the city was successively conquered by Brandenburg, the Teutonic Order, Sweden, and finally Prussia. Renamed Stettin, it was rebuilt in the middle of the nineteenth century under plans provided by Haussmann, the urban architect who remodeled Paris during the reign of Napoleon III. Heavily bombed by the Allies during World War II, it was almost totally destroyed. After the war, the city returned to Poland, with a small harbor enclave for landlocked Czechoslovakia. As in many other cities, the workers of Szczecin have repeatedly rebelled against Communist rule in Poland.

13. In early medieval times, the autopsy of human bodies was strictly prohibited. This ban was based on an abhorrence of blood by church authorities, who at that time also controlled the universities. It was only in 1238 that the Emperor Fredrick II Hohenstaufen decreed that one autopsy must be performed every five years in medical faculties. Two centuries later the edict was amended to permit one autopsy each year. Because of the prohibition of autopsy, knowledge of human anatomy was acquired from dissection of animals, which led to numerous misconceptions and errors.

14. The Gdańsk monument was erected in 1981 on the initiative of the Solidarity Trade Union to honor the shipyard workers killed in the 1970 confrontation with the Communist authorities (see note 11). The monument, which was designed and executed by workers of the shipyard, consists of three huge crosses to which anchors are attached. The crosses symbolize faith and martyrdom, whereas the anchors symbolize hope and resistance. A stylized anchor was the symbol of the Polish underground during World War II. A moving passage from a poem by Czesław Miłosz (see note 15) is inscribed at the base of the monument.

15. Czesław Miłosz is a Polish poet born in 1911 in Lithuania and educated in Wilno. An exile in France until 1951, he moved to the United States in 1961 to become professor of Slavic languages and literatures at the University of California. In 1980, he received the coveted Nobel Prize in literature, thus becoming the third Polish writer (after Henryk Sienkiewicz, 1905; and Władysław Reymont, 1924) to receive this distinction.

16. Golgotha is a hill outside the walls of the ancient city of Jerusalem also known as Calvary or "The Place of the Skulls." It was here that

the Romans carried out execution by crucifixion. On this hill, Jesus and the two thieves were crucified after being led from the Roman fortress Antonia through the streets of Jerusalem.

17. Angelo Giuseppe Roncalli (1881–1963) was ordained a priest in 1904, consecrated a bishop in 1925, and elevated to cardinal in 1953. He worked as the Apostolic Visitor to Bulgaria and Apostolic Delegate to Turkey and Greece, where he helped to build bridges of understanding between the Eastern Orthodox church and Roman Catholicism. During World War II, he saved many Jews from the holocaust by securing Portuguese passports for them. After the war he was appointed papal nuncio to France. As a cardinal and patriarch of Venice (1953), he was elected pope in 1958 to succeed Pius XII. Roncalli assumed the name John XXIII (not to be confused with the medieval antipope of the same name). His pontificate marked the beginning of a great wave of reforms (*aggiornamento*) within the Roman Catholic church, best illustrated by his calling of the Second Vatican Council (1962). His attempts to bring about peace were eloquently presented in a famous encyclical, *Pacem in Terris (Peace on Earth)*. Because of his humility and humanity he was beloved and admired by Catholics and non-Catholics alike as a spiritual leader. His death in 1963 was mourned by his admirers as well as his opponents. He was proposed for canonization in 1968.

18. Georg Wilhelm Friedrich Hegel (1770–1831) was a German theologian and philosopher and professor at the Universities of Jena (1805), Heidelberg (1816–18), and Berlin (1818–31). Hegel created a system of philosophy in which the world develops and is recognized by a process of dialectic logic. The latter consisted of a series of triads: a concept, or thesis; its opposite, or antithesis; and their derivative concept, the synthesis. His major works were *The Phenomenology of the Mind, The Science of Logic, The Encyclopedia of Philosophical Sciences,* and *The Philosophy of Right.*

19. *Gospodarz* is a Polish word that means a free man who owns and works a small or modest farm. The concept of farm includes the house, the land, other buildings, the livestock, and machinery. As head of the family, he works together with his family, and occasionally hired hands, to farm the land, produce a crop, support his family, and make a profit. The essence of this word is its encompassing nature. The *gospodarz* not only owns the farm but is its master, its warden. The responsibility for proper care and foresight is his. Success or failure revolves about his decisions and efforts. The most

accurate translation into English seems to be homesteader or crofter. The derivative words are *gospodarować* (to croft) and *gospodarstwo* (the property of a crofter).

20. Internal strife and the progressive weakness of Poland in the eighteenth-century prompted her neighbors, Russia, Prussia, and Austria, to attempt the subjugation and eventual dissolution of Poland. These adjoining states considered the existence of the Polish state to be an obstacle to their own aspirations for territorial and political expansion. Russia took the lead by initially attempting to influence the election of Polish kings and, more seriously, waging wars against Poland that were terminated by ever more stringent and demanding peace conditions. These activities resulted in three consecutive partitions in which large segments of Poland and Lithuania were detached and incorporated into the domains of Poland's neighbors. The first partition in 1772 resulted from four years of war waged by Russia against the so-called Confederation of Bar, which opposed the last Polish king elected under pressure brought to bear by Catherine the Great, empress of Russia. The second partition in 1793 ended a civil war between the populace and the Confederation of Targowica (see note 39), a confederation instigated by Russia and directly supported by Russian troops. The confederation opposed the progressive reforms embodied in the Polish constitution of May Third (see note 37). The third partition in 1795 ensued after the defeat of a national insurrection led by general Tadeusz Kościuszko (see note 44). The insurrection represented an effort to regain the territorial losses from the previous partitions. It was put down by intervening Russian and Prussian armies that massacred the civilian population of Warszawa. The third partition put an end to the independence of Poland for 123 years.

21. "Each threshold will be a bastion for us." This quotation is from the lyrics written by the poet Marja Konopnicka (1842–1910) to a patriotic song known as "Rota" that once was considered to be a second national anthem of Poland. In the words of the song she calls for a defense of the Polish language, land, and culture against the assaults of the authorities of Russia, Prussia, and Austria that partitioned Poland. In this defense, the Polish household and its threshold were the first and last lines of defense.

22. *Outpost* is the title of a novel by Bolesław Prus (1847–1912) that portrays the struggle of a Polish peasant against the onslaught of German colonists who try to buy out the land remaining in Polish hands. The novel intended to draw the attention of Polish society to

the fact that the Polish farms were dangerously weakened although, in fact, they were the most important outposts in the battle to preserve Polish identity under the conditions created by the partitioning powers (see note 20).

23. *Rola* is a Polish word that denotes tilled land as opposed to land used for pasture, gardening, or forest land. In Polish, an individual who tills the land is called a *rolnik*. The word *rola* also has another meaning that corresponds to the English word "role," that is, one's function, or a part in a play.

24. Piasts' land is a symbolic expression meaning that the land ruled by the Piast dynasty of Poland (see note 2) is forever Polish in spite of any existing political situation.

25. Socrates (469–399 B.C.) was a Greek philosopher in Athens who believed and taught that philosophy is the proper and necessary pursuit of humankind, since wisdom once acquired shall guide human behavior. Socrates held that true knowledge is identical with virtue and thus, virtue can be learned, and no one knowingly acts wrongly. In his relentless pursuit of truth, Socrates made many personal enemies and was accused of corruption and heresy. Brought to trial in Athens, he was sentenced to death.

26. Janusz Korczak (1878–1942) was the pen name of Henryk Goldszmidt, a Polish physician, writer, and educator who was of Jewish ancestry. His writings were naturalistic. Some of his best books, for example, *Child of the Salons* (1906), fell into oblivion, while others, such as *King Mattie the First* (1923), became everlasting favorites of children. Korczak was also active in health and welfare services for children as a practicing physician and director of an orphanage. Being Jewish, he and his orphanage were locked within the walls erected by the Nazis around the Warszawa Ghetto. When the Nazis began the systematic extermination of the Jews, Korczak was offered safe conduct from the Ghetto. He refused, and holding the hands of his orphans, he marched out to perish with them in the gas chambers. His life and death stand as a brilliant example of human fidelity and sacrifice.

27. "Let Poland be Poland" is a line from lyrics written by Jan Pietrzak and set to music by Włodzimierz Korcz. The song became extremely popular during the formative period of the Solidarity Movement (1980–81) and is considered to be the Solidarity anthem. The solemn words of the song tell of the everlasting and indomitable Polish spirit.

28. *Chrobry* (the Brave) is a nickname for the first crowned king of

Poland, Bolesław the Brave (992–1025, see note 2); it is pluralized
in the Polish version of Tischner's text for emphasis. His vigorous
military pursuits, the conquest of Bohemia in 1003, the war with
the German emperor, Henry II, and the conquest of Kiev (1018) all
were aimed at the creation of a federation of Slavs to counteract
German expansion. His actions were largely in vain, because during
the reign of his son and successor Poland fell under German domination that lasted until the ascendancy of his great-grandson, Bolesław the Bold (1058–1079, see note 7).

29. The name Sobieskis is the pluralized family name of King Jan
(John) III (1674–1696), once Grand Hetman of Crown (commander
in chief of the Polish army). As hetman and later as king, Jan So-
bieski repeatedly defeated the Cossacks and Turks. His greatest military feat was victory over the Turkish army that had advanced into
the very heart of Europe and laid siege to Vienna in 1683. This
victory as well as victory in the subsequent battle of Parkany put an
end to Turkish expansion in Europe and saved the Christian civili-
zation of Europe. These triumphs, however, were not able to preserve the future of Poland, which, after the death of Jan III, became
progressively weaker. About one hundred years later, Poland was
partitioned (see note 20) by the same Austria whose capital city Jan
III had saved from the onslaught of the Turks.

30. Paweł Włodkowic or Paulus Vladimiri (ca.1370–1435), a jurist and
rector of Kraków University, was a member of the Polish delegation to the Council of Constance (1414–18, see note 31). During the
debates of the Council, he argued the Polish cause in the conflict
with the Teutonic Order (see note 32), which had been recently
defeated in the decisive battle of Grunwald (see note 9). Włodkowic
argued that international policy and law should be based on the
principle that all people, even pagans, have a right to their independence and that the spread of Christianity must be accomplished
only by peaceful means. His position, which was supported by the
king of France, the rector of Paris University, the delegation Żmudz
(Samogitia), and the Ruthenian delegation, resulted in a resolution
of the Council favorable to the Polish position.

31. The Council of Constance was a council of the Roman Catholic
church called by the antipope John XXIII (1410–1415) and con-
vened in the German city of Constance to put an end to the Great
Western Schism. The schism had resulted in a parallel succession of
five popes and four antipopes. The Council sat from 1414 to 1418
and was organized around national caucuses (Germany, Italy,

France, etc.) In 1415, the Council promulgated the Articles of Constance affirming that it was the supreme authority within the Church and thus, by implication, in Europe. Following this edict, two of the antipopes, John XXIII (1410–1415) and Benedict XIII (1394–1417), were deposed, and Gregory XII (1406–1415) was recognized as the true pope. Gregory resigned in a short time, and a new pope, Martin V (1417–1431), was elected and recognized. Martin V ratified all the reforms proposed by the Council except the assertion that the Council had supreme power, exceeding that of the pope himself. Having settled the issue of the papacy, the Council next undertook to settle the arguments between nations and rulers, such as those between France and Burgundy and between Poland and the Teutonic Order. The Council further tried and burned at the stake the Czech religious reformer Jan Hus, in spite of having given him an earlier guarantee of safe conduct to appear before the Council and defend himself.

32. The Teutonic Order, originally known as the brethren of a hospital at Acre, was founded by Crusaders in 1190; subsequently it was raised to a military order of knighthood under the name of the Order of Knights of the Hospital of St. Mary of the Teutons in Jerusalem. The order was composed for the most part of German knights and possessed a monastic character, including vows of poverty, chastity, and obedience. Eventually, the Grand Masters of the Order attempted to establish a territorial domain with political as well as religious authority. The Order remained in Jerusalem from 1191 until 1221, when, frustrated by the kingdom of Jerusalem in their attempts to establish a domain, they removed to Hungary. The Order had been invited to Hungary by King Andrew II to fight against the Cumans. Here they remained until 1224. In 1226 they were invited by Prince Konrad (Conrad) of Mazovia of the Piast dynasty to oppose the incursions of the Prussians, at the time pagans. The members of the Order became known as the Knights of Cross because of the black cross on their white capes. Konrad gave the castle of Chełmno to the Order and permitted them to retain any lands that they could take from the Prussians, with the understanding that both the castle and acquired lands would remain under Konrad's suzerainty. The Order immediately took steps to avoid these conditions by founding its own stronghold at Toruń (1230), securing a charter from the German emperor, placing itself under papal authority, and making an alliance with a similar order, "The Brothers of the Sword," that had recently settled in Livonia.

Having established itself, the Order subsequently refused any obedience to the Mazovian prince. The Order then set about establishing its own state by exterminating the Prussians and settling the conquered land with German immigrants. The Order also secured a papal license for trade in 1263, took the ancient seaport town of Gdańsk (see note 11), and built a new stronghold at Malbork (Marienburg). After conquering Prussia and Pomerania, the Order began to look southward, invading and annexing Polish provinces (1331–32). Even when ordered by a papal court to return the lands to Poland, the Order refused to obey and began attacks on Samogitia and Lithuania. All of these actions precipitated a reaction in the form of a war that ended in the defeat of the Order at the Battle of Grunwald in 1410 (see note 9). However, it required three more wars to bring the Order to the second Treaty of Toruń in 1466 that forced the Order to cede all lands but a part of Prussia to Poland. Prussia then became a fiefdom of Poland with its capital in Królewiec (Königsberg). The Order became a secular principality when its last Grand Master, Albrecht von Hohenzollern, became a Protestant in 1525, paying official homage to the Polish monarch. This secular duchy was later to become the kingdom of Prussia, which would eventually participate in the partition of Poland in the late eighteenth century (see note 20).

33. Mikołaj Kopernik (Nicolaus Copernicus, 1473–1543) was the son of a Toruń burgher. Educated at the Universities of Kraków and Padua, he settled in Frombork in the province of Warmia and became canon of the cathedral, a physician, and an astronomer. Finding that his own observations did not agree with the ancient Ptolemaic theory of planetary motion, he proposed a new system in which the geocentric organization of the solar system was replaced by a heliocentric structure. Although some parts of the Copernican system were still incorrect, his ideas paved the way for Kepler's laws of planetary motion and Newton's law of gravity. His monumental work entitled *De revolutionibus orbium coelestium* was published in 1543 and was dedicated to Pope Paul III by the author who was then on his death bed.

34. Andrzej Frycz Modrzewski (ca. 1503–1572) was one of the greatest Polish, if not one of the greatest European, social thinkers of the sixteenth century. A jurist, courtier, and royal secretary, he wrote in Latin. His social concepts and propositions reflected the idea of the equality of all in the eyes of the law. His concept of the same penalty for a given crime regardless of the perpetrator or the victim (*De*

poena homicidii, 1543) was two hundred years ahead of existing European jurisprudence. His major work *Comentarii de republica emendanda,* 1551, consisted of a description of an ideal state in which an individual's rights, within limits, were to be subjugated to the greater good of society. According to his concept, the state should be involved in the welfare of the elderly and in social education. His ideas were so far ahead of his time that he was understood by neither Poles nor foreigners, neither Catholics nor Protestants. He himself was a member of the Polish brethren (Aryan) church, a radical sect of Protestantism based on Calvinism. His full and uncensored works were published in Polish translation only in 1577, after his death.

35. The Commission of National Education was an institution created by the Polish Diet in 1773 and represented the first ministry of public education in Europe. It replaced the educational system that had been run by the Jesuit Order until its dissolution by Pope Clement XIV (1773). Using funds acquired from the dissolved Order of Jesuits, the Commission elaborated a system of national education that encompassed both primary schools and universities. The program was strongly influenced by the educational ideals of the Order of Piarists. In general, it gave priority to moral and practical training over religious instruction. The Commission aimed at preparing students for their future civic duties. The work of the Commission was encouraged and supported by King Stanisław August Poniatowski, a great patron of the arts and sciences.

36. Karol Wojtyła, born in 1920, was initially a student of philology, literature, and theater, and later became a laborer and member of the resistance underground during the Nazi occupation of Poland. In 1942, he decided to become a priest and studied theology while hiding in the palace of the archbishop of Kraków. Ordained in 1946, he was consecrated a bishop in 1958, appointed archbishop of Kraków in 1964, and named a cardinal in 1967. During this time he was simultaneously climbing the steps of a scholarly career, becoming a lecturer and then chairman of the Department of Ethics at the Catholic University of Lublin. Even as a prominent churchman and scientist, he found time to write poetry and plays. His religious, social, and literary activities earned him the love and respect of the citizens of Kraków and eventually wider recognition through trips abroad—both religious and political. Perhaps his most important trip was a journey to Germany where, with the Polish primate Stefan Cardinal Wyszyński, he brought a message of Christian forgive-

ness and reconciliation from the people of Poland to the Germans. He was active in the work of the Second Vatican Council and drew the attention of many churchmen. In 1978, he was elected pope, assuming the name John Paul II in honor of his three immediate predecessors. Presently, he is known throughout the world as the people's pope who brings a message of love, understanding, hope, and justice for all humanity. For the Poles, he is also a symbol of their highest hopes for freedom as well as their true spiritual leader.

37. The Constitution of May Third, 1791, the first true Polish constitution, was promulgated by the "Four-Year" or "Great" Diet (1788–92). The document, which was approved on May 3, 1791, was modeled in many respects on the recent American constitution of 1776. The constitution gave to the burghers the same rights enjoyed by the nobility and took the peasants under the protection of the government, although it stopped short of abolishing serfdom. Furthermore, the act made the Polish throne hereditary in the house of Saxony, thus ending the foreign influences that had occurred during previous elections, and it abolished the principle of *liberum veto* (blockage of a measure by a single vote). Together with an earlier resolution to form a standing army of a hundred thousand, the constitution was an enormous step forward toward the salvation of Poland from imminent collapse under the Russian threat. Unfortunately, the counterreaction that it elicited from Russia led to military intervention that ended in the second partition (1793, see note 20). The anniversary of the constitution has always been the national holiday of Poland, even after official celebration of this day was abolished by the Communist regime, which considers it too strong a reminder of anti-Russian feelings.

38. The last king of the Vasa dynasty, Jan Kazimierz (John Casimir, 1648–1668) after defeating an attempted invasion of Poland by the Cossacks, was initially unsuccessful in turning back an invasion by the Swedes and was forced to flee the country. Returning from exile in 1656, he made a solemn vow in the cathedral of Lwów that the Blessed Virgin Mary was to be eternally recognized as the Queen of Poland and the Queen of the monarchs of Poland. This proclamation has remained valid through the ages, and indeed, these royal vows were reaffirmed by the Polish people three hundred years later on the anniversary of the successful defense against the Swedes of the shrine of the Black Madonna at Częstochowa.

39. With the instigation and support of Empress Catharine the Great of Russia, a small group of Polish nobility illegally formed the Confed-

eration of Targowica in 1792 to oppose actively the recently passed Constitution of May Third (see note 37). The Russian army immediately invaded Poland under the pretext of being invited to help the confederates. Initially, the Russian army was repelled by Polish forces led by Józef Poniatowski and Tadeusz Kościuszko (see note 44), but ultimately the king and many other nobles joined the Confederation, believing that an agreement with Russia could be negotiated. Unfortunately, in the end this turned out to be only wishful thinking, because Russia forced the second partition (see note 20) and its approval by the so-called Silent Diet of Grodno. This was the last diet of an independent Poland, and it sat silent surrounded by Russian soldiers.

40. The University of Kraków was founded in 1364 by Kazimierz the Great for the most part as a law faculty modeled after similar faculties in Italy. After the king's death in 1370, and during the reign of Louis of Anjou (1370–1382, see note 2) and Queen Jadwiga (1384–1399, see note 3), the university fell into decline. It was renovated and reformed by King Władysław Jagiełło in 1400 (see note 3), who used the jewelry of the late queen to finance the reformation of the university. Since that time the university has been called Jagiellonian. In the six hundred and more years of its existence, it has become a center of European education as well as the center of Polish science and culture. It has produced a host of internationally prominent scientists, scholars, and statesmen.

41. Jan Kochanowski (1530–1584) was probably the greatest poet of the Polish Renaissance and elevated the level of Polish literature to that of the rest of Europe. He was the first writer to use the Polish language exclusively in his work and is often considered the father of literary Polish. Educated in Kraków and Padua in the Italian and French tradition, he went on to create his own unique style. Initially a royal courtier with an ambition to become a priest, he relinquished these ideas to become a country squire. In his philosophy and writing, he rose above the religious conflicts of the time and befriended both Catholics and Protestants. He was also the first to introduce erotic poetry into Polish literature. Among his most important works are *Trifles, The Psalms of David* (translated from the Bible), and *Threnos*. In this last work, written under the influence of grief after the death of a daughter, he made a great contribution to literature in general by presenting the conflict of philosophy and the emotions in a manner comparable to the ancient Greek tragedies of Sophocles.

42. Piotr Skarga (1536–1612), a Jesuit and politician, was for many years the royal chaplain and confessor to King Zygmunt III Vasa. An excellent orator and linguist, he published a collection of his sermons in a treatise, *Sermons in the Diets* (1597), that discussed the flaws of the Polish political system and suggested means for correcting them. He, indeed, predicted the future catastrophe of the partitions (see note 20). A great patriot and man of courage, Skarga had the foresight to observe and proclaim his vision of his beloved country. Skarga was a major architect of the reconciliation between the Ruthenian Orthodox and the Roman Catholic Churches that in 1595–96 culminated in the formation of the Uniate or the Ukrainian Catholic Church at the Union of Brześć (Brest). Toward the end of World War II this church was officially suppressed by the Soviet government and its members were forcibly incorporated into the Russian Orthodox Church, while its hierarchy was imprisoned or killed. Presently, the Ukrainian Catholic Church exists in Poland and in North America. Skarga showed no tolerance for the spread of the ideas of the Protestant Reformation in Poland, nor for the separation of secular power from the church.

43. The Manifesto of Połaniec was issued on May 7th, 1794, in an army camp near the village of Połaniec by Tadeusz Kościuszko (see note 44), the leader of a national insurrection against the Russians. The manifesto declared freedom for all peasants and the immediate abolition of serfdom for those who would take up arms against the Russian invaders. In a sense, this declaration was an extension of the Constitution of May Third (see note 37) that left the issue of serfdom unresolved. Unfortunately, it came too late to have sufficient impact on most peasants and failed to incite their wide participation. The insurrection was defeated, and the third partition of Poland quickly followed in 1795.

44. Tadeusz Kościuszko (1746–1817) was a military engineer trained in the Cadets' Corps of Warszawa and military school of Paris at the personal expense of King Stanisław August Poniatowski. Inspired by the ideals of the struggle against foreign oppressors, he traveled to America in 1777. He was introduced to General George Washington, to whom he offered his services against the British. He fortified the Bemis Heights (under General Gates) and West Point (1778) and fought in the Carolinas (1780). After his discharge from the American forces as a brigadier general and being made a honorary citizen of the United States, Kościuszko returned to Poland to fight against the Russians, who at that time were attempting the

second partition (see note 20). In 1794, he issued a call for a national insurrection and vowed in the marketplace of Kraków not to rest until the sovereignty and borders of Poland were secured. With an initial force of four-thousand men, he challenged the joint forces of Russia and Prussia. After some victories, he was defeated, seriously wounded, and taken prisoner at the Battle of Maciejowice. Eventually freed by the Russian Emperor Paul I, Kościuszko returned to America, where he freed all the slaves on a plantation that had been awarded to him by an act of Congress. Returning once more to Europe, he settled in Solothurn, Switzerland. Kościuszko refused to support the movement of Napoleon I, since he doubted Napoleon's intentions. Still, in 1815, after the fall of Napoleon, Kościuszko pleaded with the Russian Emperor Alexander I to preserve the Duchy of Warszawa created by Napoleon. He died in exile, and his remains were transferred to Poland only after it regained its independence in 1918. The urn with his heart rested in the Warszawa cathedral until 1939, when it was removed to save it from the hands of the invading Nazis. The urn was kept for many years in the vaults of a Canadian bank but was finally returned to Poland, where it rests in a separate hall of the National Museum. Visiting school children leave their school badges beneath the urn as a pledge to his ideals of freedom and independence.

45. The Wisła (Vistula) River is the longest river in Poland (655 miles). In its run, it crosses the entire country, beginning in the Tatra Mountains (see note 46) in the south and emptying into the Gdańsk Gulf of the Baltic Sea in the north. It collects many tributaries along its run: the Dunajec, San, Narew, Bug, Wieprz, and the Noteć. It also passes through such ancient cities as Kraków, Kazimierz, Warszawa, Bydgoszcz, Toruń, Malbork, Tczew, and Gdańsk.

46. The Tatra Mountains (Tatras) are the highest range within the Carpathian Mountains. The Tatras lie on the border of Poland and Czechoslovakia and are located in both countries (High Tatras) or in Slovakia only (Low Tatras). The central portion of the range is currently a national preserve that spans the frontiers of the two nations. The Tatras are inhabited by fiercely independent highlanders, *górale,* who could not be totally subjugated even by the Nazis.

47. Cyprian Kamil Norwid (1921–1883) was the most tragic and least known poet of the Polish Romantic era. After living through the November Uprising (1930–31, see note 51) and the period of Russian repression that followed, he voluntarily left Poland in 1842. Traveling through Germany, Italy, and America, he finally settled

in Paris in 1854. Misunderstood and alienated from his contemporaries, Norwid wrote largely for himself, and generally his works remained unknown. Only recently have all his works been collected and published with scholarly commentaries. He died penniless as a ward of the Paris Hospice of Saint Casimir and was buried in an unmarked paupers' grave of unknown location.

48. Zygmunt Krasiński (1812–1859) for most of his life wrote under a pen name to avoid conflict with his father, who was a collaborator with the Russian authorities who then occupied Poland. His constant fear of being exposed is reflected in the manner of his writing and his attitudes. However, he is often considered the most sophisticated Polish poet of the Romantic era. In his most famous work, *The Undivine Comedy,* he showed in a symbolic way the approaching revolution and inevitable demise of his own social class, the nobility. In another work, *Irydion,* he confronted the problem of conspiracy as well as the topic of original and repeated sins, in a manner comparable to Milton's *Paradise Lost.*

49. *Redemptor hominis* or *The Redeemer of Mankind* was the first encyclical of Pope John Paul II, issued on March 4, 1979. It consists of four chapters that outline the views and ideals of the pope on the Catholic doctrine of faith, the social aspects of faith, and the mission of the Church. Its leading theme is the dignity of each human being as the child of God. Some suggest that the name "Solidarity" had been inspired by the appeal for acting together contained in the encyclical.

50. At present, His Eminence Józef Cardinal Glemp is the primate. Traditionally, the archbishop of Gniezno and Warszawa is the primate of Poland. In the past, the primate was the regent (*inter rex*) during the period between the death of one monarch and the election of his successor. The role of the primate as the spiritual leader of Poland was recently confirmed by the heroic stand of the late Stefan Cardinal Wyszyński, who was admired by virtually all Poles and was an authority with whom the Communists had to reckon.

51. The Congress of Vienna (1815) created from the Duchy of Warszawa a constitutional Kingdom of Poland, with the Russian emperors as kings. However, neither Alexander I nor Nicholas I intended to observe the constitution of this kingdom. On the contrary, both Governor General Novosilcov and the commander of the army, Grand Duke Constantine, brutally suppressed any sign of independence. When the Poles learned that the Russians intended to use the Polish army to suppress the Paris revolution of

1830 and the independence struggle of the Belgians, the Uprising started, on November 29, 1830. The cadets of the military academy attacked the residence of the grand duke, forcing him to flee. The insurrection rapidly spread and became the formal Polish-Russian war of 1830–31. Militarily well-motivated and enthusiastic, the army was led by a succession of commanders who, although well-intentioned, lacked the capability and coordination to succeed. During the war, the Polish Diet declared the Russian emperor deposed from the throne of Poland and elected Adam Czartoryski, a well-known statesman, as head of state, but it failed to come to grips with the question of serfdom. The uprising ended after eleven months, as Warsaw fell to the Russians and the remnants of the army either capitulated or went into exile. Some groups of exiled soldiers were hailed as messengers of freedom as they made their way through revolutionary Europe. The fleeing soldiers were soon followed by many politicians and artists, who left Poland to escape a brutal Russian persecution. The Russian post-war reign of terror sent many Poles to Siberia and led to the suspension of the consitution and the closing of the universities.

52. Pięć Stawów (Five Lakes) are five deep lakes situated in a valley of the same name in the High Tatras (see note 46). The area is a beautiful and unspoiled recreation spot.

53. An encyclical *Laborem exercens, On Human Work,* was issued by Pope John Paul II on September 14, 1981. It is a philosophical and theological reflection on the situation of the worker in the contemporary world.

54. Pharisaism is a religious movement that originated in Palestine about 135 B.C. Its followers assigned great importance to the strict observance of Jewish Law, both oral and written. Current use of the term refers to the extremely legalistic and casuistic approach represented by many, but not all, groups within Pharisaism. Although often the object of criticism from opposing religious groups (Sadducees and, later, Christians), Pharisaism established religious rules and traditions that were continued by Orthodox Judaism (since about A.D. 135). Christianity, too, adopted significant theological insights from Pharisaism.

55. The Napoleonic wars were a series of military endeavors by Napoleon Bonaparte, first as Director (1799), later as First Consul (1802), and finally as Emperor of France. Wars with Austria, England, Haiti, Prussia, Russia, Sweden, the Papal States, and Spain resulted in a political reorganization of Europe. By conquering and

subjugating various states and placing members of his family or entourage on their thrones, Napoleon succeeded in incorporating some countries into France. Belgium, Holland, the Papal States, and the Illyrian Provinces were all annexed to France in this way. Still others, the Duchy of Warszawa, Prussia, Austria, Denmark, and Norway were brought into alliance with France. Other states were simply dominated by the threat of French military prowess. These included: Italy, Naples, and the German Confederation of the Rhine. The new order in Europe collapsed after Napoleon invaded Russia in 1812. After reaching Moscow, the French army, although undefeated in battle, was forced to retreat in the middle of winter. During the withdrawal, Napoleon's Grand Army of over half a million men was decimated. The remnants of this army and fresh troops from France faced a coalition of forces from Russia, Prussia, Austria, and England in the Battle of Nations near Leipzig in 1813 and were decisively defeated. The victorious coalition then marched on Paris and forced the abdication of Napoleon, who was then exiled to the island of Elba.